Cultural And Geographical Exploration

Ancient Civilizations of the Aztecs and Maya

CHRONICLES FROM *NATIONAL GEOGRAPHIC*

Cultural And Geographical Exploration

Cultural And Geographical Exploration

Ancient Civilizations of the Aztecs and Maya

CHRONICLES FROM *NATIONAL GEOGRAPHIC*

Arthur M. Schlesinger, jr.
Senior Consulting Editor

Fred L. Israel
General Editor

CHELSEA HOUSE PUBLISHERS

Philadelphia

CHELSEA HOUSE PUBLISHERS

Editor in Chief Stephen Reginald
Managing Editor James D. Gallagher
Production Manager Pamela Loos
Art Director Sara Davis
Director of Photography Judy L. Hasday
Senior Production Editor Lisa Chippendale

First Printing

1 3 5 7 9 8 6 4 2

Library of Congress Cataloging-in-Publication Data

Ancient Civilizations of the Aztecs and Maya / Arthur M. Schlesinger, Jr.,
Senior consulting editor; Fred L. Israel, general editor.
p.   cm. — (Cultural and geographical exploration)
Includes bibliographical references and index.
ISBN 0-7910-5103-X (HC)
1. Mayas.   2. Aztecs.   3. Mexico—Antiquities.   4. Central
America—Antiquities.   I . Schlesinger, Arthur Meier, 1917–
II. Israel, Fred L.   III. National Geographic Society (U.S.)
IV. Series.
F1435.A625   1999
972—dc21   98-47476
                                                                CIP

CONTENTS

"THE GREATEST EDUCATIONAL JOURNAL"

When the first *National Geographic* magazine appeared in October 1888, the United States totaled 38 states. Grover Cleveland was President. The nation's population hovered around 60 million. Great Britain's Queen Victoria also ruled as the Empress of India. William II became Kaiser of Germany that year. Tsar Alexander III ruled Russia and the Turkish Empire stretched from the Balkans to the tip of Arabia. To Westerners, the Far East was still a remote and mysterious land. Throughout the world, riding the back of an animal was the principle means of transportation. Unexplored and unmarked places dotted the global map.

On January 13, 1888, thirty-three men—scientists, cartographers, inventors, scholars, and explorers—met in Washington, D. C. They had accepted an invitation from Gardiner Greene Hubbard (1822-1897), the first president of the Bell Telephone Co. and a leader in the education of the deaf, to form the National Geographic Society "to increase and diffuse geographic knowledge." One of the assembled group noted that they were the "first explorers of the Grand Canyon and the Yellowstone, those who had carried the American flag farthest north, who had measured the altitude of our famous mountains, traced the windings of our coasts and rivers, determined the distribution of flora and fauna, enlightened us in the customs of the aborigines, and marked out the path of storm and flood." Nine months later, the first issue of *National Geographic* magazine was sent out to 165 charter members. Today, more than a century later, membership has grown to an astounding 11 million in more than 170 nations. Several times that number regularly read the monthly issues of the *National Geographic* magazine.

The first years were difficult ones for the new magazine. The earliest volumes seem dreadfully scientific and quite dull. The articles in Volume I, No. 1 set the tone—W. M Davis, "Geographic Methods in Geologic Investigation," followed by W. J. McGee, "The Classification of Geographic Forms by Genesis." Issues came out erratically—three in 1889, five in 1890, four in 1891; and two in 1895. In January 1896 "an illustrated monthly" was added to the title. The November issue that year contained a photograph of a half-naked Zulu bride and bridegroom in their wedding finery staring full face into the camera. But, a reader must have wondered what to make of the accompanying text: "These people . . . possess some excellent traits, but are horribly cruel when once they have smelled blood." In hopes of expanding circulation, the Board of Managers offered newsstand copies at \$.25 each and began to accept advertising. But the magazine essentially remained unchanged. Circulation only rose slightly.

In January 1898, shortly after Gardiner Greene Hubbard's death, his son-in-law Alexander Graham Bell (1847-1922) agreed to succeed him as the second president of the National Geographic Society. Bell invented the telephone in 1876 and, while pursuing his life long goal of improving the lot of the deaf, had turned his amazingly versatile mind to contemplating such varied problems as human flight, air conditioning, and popularizing geography. The society then had about 1100 members—the magazine was on the edge of bankruptcy. Bell did not want the job. He wrote in his diary though that he accepted leadership of the Society "in order to save it. Geography is a fascinating subject and it can be made interesting," he told the board of directors. Bell abandoned the unsuccessful attempt to increase circulation through newsstand sales. "Our journal," he wrote "should go to members, people who believe in our work and want to help." He understood that the lure for prospective members should be an association with a society that made it possible for the average person to share with kings and scientists the excitement of sending an expedition to a strange land or an explorer to an inaccessible region. This idea, more than any other, has been responsible for the growth of the National Geographic Society and for the popularity of the magazine. "I can well remember," recalled Bell in 1912, "how the idea was laughed at that we should ever reach a membership of ten thousand." That year it had soared to 107,000!

Bell attributed this phenomenal growth though to one man who had transformed the *National Geographic* magazine into "the greatest educational journal in the world"—Gilbert H. Grosvenor (1875-1966). Bell had hired the then 24-year-old Grosvenor in 1899 as the Society's first full-time employee "to put some life into the magazine." He personally escorted the new editor, who will become his son-in-law, to the Society's headquarters—a small rented room shared with the American Forestry Association on the fifth floor of a building, long since gone, across 15th street from the U. S. Treasury in downtown Washington. Grosvenor remembered the headquarters "littered with old magazines, newspapers, and a few record books and six enormous boxes crammed with *Geographics* returned by the newsstands." "No desk!" exclaimed Bell. "I'll send you mine." That afternoon, delivery men brought Grosvenor a large walnut rolltop and the new editor began to implement Bell's instructions—to transform the magazine from one of cold geographic fact "expressed in hieroglyphic terms which the layman could not understand into a vehicle for carrying the living, breathing, human-interest truth about this great world of ours to the people." And what did Bell consider appropriate "geographic subjects?" He replied: "The world and all that is in it is our theme."

Grosvenor shared Bell's vision of a great society and magazine which would disseminate geographic knowledge. "I thought of geography in terms of its Greek root: *geographia*—a description of the world," he later wrote. "It thus becomes the most catholic of subjects, universal in appeal, and embracing nations, people, plants, birds, fish. We would never lack interesting subjects." To attract readers, Grosvenor had to change the public attitude toward geography which he knew was regarded as "one of the dullest of all subjects, something to inflict upon schoolboys and avoid in later life." He wondered why certain books which relied heavily on geographic description remained popular—Charles Darwin's *Voyage of the Beagle*, Richard Dana, Jr.'s *Two Years Before the Mast* and even Herodotus' *History*. Why did readers for generations, and with Herodotus' travels, for twenty centuries return to these books? What did these volumes, which used so many geographic descriptions, have in common? What was the secret? According to Grosvenor, the answer was that "each was an accurate, eyewitness, firsthand account. Each contained simple straightforward writing—writing that sought to make pictures in the reader's mind."

Gilbert Grosvenor was editor of the *National Geographic* magazine for 55 years, from 1899 until 1954. Each of the 660 issues under his direction had been a highly readable geography textbook. He took Bell's vision and made it a reality. Acclaimed as "Mr. Geography," he discovered the earth anew for himself and for millions around the globe. He charted the dynamic course which the National Geographic Society and its magazine followed for more than half a century. In so doing, he forged an instrument for world education and understanding unique in this or any age. Under his direction, the *National Geographic* magazine grew from a few hundred copies—he recalled carrying them to the post office on his back—to more than five million at the time of his retirement as editor, enough for a stack 25 miles high.

This Chelsea House series celebrates Grosvenor's first twenty-five years as editor of the *National Geographic*. "The mind must see before it can believe," said Grosvenor. From the earliest days, he filled the magazine with photographs and established another Geographic principle—to portray people in their natural attire or lack of it. Within his own editorial committee, young Grosvenor encountered the prejudice that photographs had to be "scientific." Too often, this meant dullness. To Grosvenor, every picture and sentence had to be interesting to the layman. "How could you educate and inform if you lost your audience by boring your readers?" Grosvenor would ask his staff. He persisted and succeeded in making the *National Geographic* magazine reflect this fascinating world.

To the young-in-heart of every age there is magic in the name *National Geographic*. The very words conjure up enchanting images of faraway places, explorers and scientists, sparkling seas and dazzling mountain peaks, strange plants, animals, people, and customs. The small society founded in 1888 "for the increase and diffusion of geographic knowledge" grew, under the guidance of one man, to become a great force for knowledge and understanding. This achievement lies in the genius of Gilbert H. Grosvenor, the architect and master builder of the National Geographic Society and its magazine.

Fred L. Israel
The City College of the City University of New York

ANCIENT CIVILIZATIONS

FRED L. ISRAEL

THE MAYA

The ancient Maya and Aztecs created two of the most magnificent civilizations of pre-Columbian America. The Mayan culture arose, flourished, and vanished in less than a thousand years, reaching its peak between 250 A.D. and 900 A.D. The Maya lived in Central America and south Mexico, and their horizons reached to the Valley of Mexico in the west and to Panama in the east. Their civilization progressed without contact with European or Asian civilizations, although they were influenced by events within their geographic sphere. In spite of their relative isolation, the Maya produced a remarkable architecture and excelled in painting and sculpture.

The height of Mayan civilization, 250 A.D.–900 A.D., is referred to as the Classical Period. It is during this time that the Maya developed their great cities. The largest cities included tens of thousands of inhabitants. Many smaller sites existed as well. These may have been independent or vassals to a larger city. Small towns, villages, even isolated farms have all been found.

Archaeologists have concluded that the society was organized politically into rival city-states, all sharing the same civilization—language, art, farming techniques, and so forth. It was an intensely competitive society, full of wars, annexations, and alliances. In each large city, the king was the equivalent of a god, responsible to his people for the successful functioning of the universe. To impress his subjects and his rivals, each city-state ruler tried to live in a sumptuous palace. Rulers also built tall limestone pyramids with small temples at the top. There, priests performed religious ceremonies.

Although Mayan glyphs have been deciphered, so much is still unknown about these people. It is known, however, that religion played a central part in their daily lives. Each day had special religious importance, and religious festivals took place throughout the year. To obtain the help of the gods, the Maya fasted, prayed, and offered animal and human sacrifices. They frequently offered their own blood to the deities. They probably used hallucinogenic drugs made from mushrooms, and the influence of drugs may account for some of the more bizarre Mayan rituals.

At first, scholars assumed that the abundant carvings in the countless monuments were either religious symbols or notations denoting the movement of planets. However, with the realization in the mid-1980s that the glyphs constituted an actual language of complex words, it was possible to understand inscriptions throughout the Mayan realm. As a result, the romantic conjecture of a peaceful society has now given way to the view that the Maya were warring nations who tortured and sometimes sacrificed their captives. The Mayan writings have now become the most important source for understanding their civilization.

For reasons still unknown, the Maya abandoned their cities about 900 A.D. They dispersed to the Yucatan and the highlands of Guatamala. In these areas, the Maya continued to prosper until Spain conquered them in the mid-1500s.

THE AZTECS

The Aztecs were a native American Indian people who ruled a mighty empire in Mexico during the 1400s and early 1500s A.D. Their empire was conquered by the Spaniards in 1521, but Aztec culture has left a lasting mark on the Mexican way of life.

The Aztec empire was established in less than a century. It encompassed the Valley of Mexico, a huge oval basin about 7500 feet above sea level. Although the valley is in the tropics, its high altitude gave it a mild climate. The land was divided into numerous small states. Eventually, the entire area was united under an emperor who had great powers but whose primary function was to command the army. He ruled with a council of nobles, whom he consulted before making important decisions. Tribute was paid to the emperor by subject towns and included materials such as gold, silver, live birds, precious stones, bales of cotton, and woven blankets.

The Aztecs were fierce warriors who believed it their duty to sacrifice the people they captured in battle to their gods. On a gentler side, the Aztecs also composed music, wrote poetry, and were skilled in medicine. The calendar became the Aztec symbol and was usually shown with a human face, with its tongue hanging out. This has been interpreted as Tonatiuh, the sun god, demanding offerings of human blood.

Religion was extremely important in Aztec life. They were terrified by the forces of nature, which they could not understand. The Aztec worshiped many gods and goddesses, each of whom ruled one or more human activities or aspects of nature. There were several hundred religious festivals held each year to appease the gods. Since the Aztec economy was based on farming, there were many agricultural divinities, with the sun-god being the most powerful one. The most enviable fate was to die in combat or on a sacrificial stone. They believed that by this blood sacrifice—which contributed to the sun's red glow—one would join the sun in its fruitful march around the universe.

When the Spanish arrived in Tenochtitlan, the Aztec capital, they were impressed by the beauty, order, and cleanliness of this city of 150,000–300,000 inhabitants. Its size ranked it as one of the largest metropolises in the world at the time. This favorable impression vanished when they reached the great ceremonial center. The immense enclosure contained several dozen temples, the largest being the Great Temple. The Spaniards were shocked by the blood-soaked steps and the terrible smell. In fact, the inauguration of the Great Temple in 1487 was celebrated with splendid festivals where thousands of victims were sacrificed in four days.

Little Aztec architecture remains, as the Spanish considered it their Christian duty to wipe out all traces of the Aztec religion. They destroyed the capital city and built Mexico City on the ruins. However, archaeologists have excavated the site of the Great Temple in downtown Mexico City, recovering thousands of objects, including jewelry and pottery as well as the remains of human and animal sacrifices.

VOL. XXIV, No. 3　　WASHINGTON　　MARCH, 1913

MYSTERIOUS TEMPLES OF THE JUNGLE
The Prehistoric Ruins of Guatemala

By W. F. SANDS

FORMERLY AMERICAN MINISTER TO GUATEMALA

WITH the opening of the Quirigua ruins in Guatemala a most important addition is being made to the material now available for study of the races which once occupied the low, hot coast land between Copán, in Honduras, through the Guatemala littoral, Petén, and Quintana Roo to Yucatan.

Master races they were as were once the Brahmans in Indo-China. They conquered in easy battle the fever-ridden natives, and lived thenceforth upon the country and its population.

They taught them nothing of their higher civilization, but ground them back to the earth, until inbreeding, idleness, and fever took their toll, and in their turn they were overthrown and perished, leaving nothing but the elaborate monuments and massive buildings which, covered with the mould of centuries of quick springing and quick decaying tropical forest, form the "Indian mounds" so plentiful in this region.

A RACE OF PRIESTLY CONQUERORS

The theory of an alien sacerdotal aristocracy, claiming divine descent because of superior development, and ruling an untutored conquered race, while it offers no suggestion as to origin, may at least explain why no memory of their rule remains among the inhabitants of these regions today. Knowledge of every kind was kept from the subject races, and with the downfall the slave fled from the ancient holy places, and the symbols of arrogance, cruelty, and power were shunned for centuries as an abomination.

It is not necessary to hold with Brasseur de Bourbourg that all these countries (the "Hinterland" of Atlantis) were submerged when the is-

THE BEAUTIFUL SITUATION OF QUIRIGUA

"The ruins lie on low, flat land, flooded and renewed each rainy season by the Motagua's overflow—rich, inexhaustible alluvial soil, and ideal for banana-growing. A more inspiring spot can hardly be imagined. Under the immense ceiba and other coast trees (70 and 80 feet to the lowest branches, each as big as a 30-year maple and hung with orchids or Spanish moss) has grown up a thicket of palms and fern trees, forming, when the underbrush is cleared, arching forest galleries impossible to describe" (see text, page 11).

land-continent was destroyed, although his theory is immensely attractive, and that after remaining under the sea for an unknown period they rose once more and were peopled from the highlands.

It is simpler to imagine, as long as we have nothing definite to go on and one man's tale is as good as another's, that some such catastrophe took place as is so charmingly suggested in Sir Hugh Clifford's "Tragedy of Angkor," and that the degenerate rulers of the coast were shown suddenly to their subjects by some attack of the hardier mountain tribes to be no longer irresistible, no longer divine, but only very feeble men, and so were wiped out as utterly and effectually as would have been the first weak settlement on our own shores without succor from the mother country.

AN ENVOY
WHO FAILED TO FIND HIS GOAL

Perhaps none of the ruins of America is more accessible now to Americans than those of Quirigua; and yet, though frequently visited, they are among the least known.

John Stevens, in his gossipy "Travels in Central America, etc.," in 1839, has left an excellent account of both Quirigua and its neighbor, Copán, during his wanderings in search of a Federal government sufficiently stable to receive his credentials as American Minister.

Failing in the object of his official mission, he returned north through the Guatemalan highlands, visiting also the ruined cities of Quiché, and so up the ridge of the Cordillera, through Chiapas to Palenque and down to Chichen, Itza, and Uxmal, in Yucatan—a wonderfully beautiful journey and not in any way difficult for a saddle-hardened rider.

Stevens left a valuable record; but his real treasure (aside from the personal reminiscence of the astonishing Carrera, who from a particularly brutal swineherd became a demi-god and one of the ablest rulers Guatemala has known) is the series of admirable drawings by Catherwood, who accompanied him, of all the monuments in both Quirigua and Copán, which remain unexcelled even by photography.

Many travelers have passed through since the completion of the railway; but, with the exception of Maudslay, none has attempted to give more than such a description as I am now writing. At present all men are equal, for no one has

succeeded in deciphering the historical writings of Quirigua.

THE SITE OF QUIRIGUA CLEARED

In the spring of 1910 the tract of land surrounding the monuments, on the left bank of the Motagua River, was opened for planting by the United Fruit Company of Boston, and a park left about the principal ruins. The company generously supplied labor and many other facilities for clearing this park of underbrush and cleaning the stones, so that at last an organized study was made possible, under the guidance and supervision of Prof. Edgar L. Hewett (Director of the School of American Archeology, at Santa Fé, New Mexico) and of Mr. Sylvanus Griswold Morley.

Both of these gentlemen have spent many months in exploration and detailed examination, and under Mr. Hewett's able direction the institute has an opportunity for study hardly paralleled in the history of American archeological research.

Quirigua should become the starting point, the workshop, and the school for beginners in this branch until the gradual development of the country makes organized extension possible into Petén without the hardships and risks to health and life to which sojourners in that beautiful but treacherous country are now subject. Quirigua is free from all these drawbacks, and nothing could be easier than its approach.

The steamer that brings the traveler from New Orleans is only one entire day out of sight of land. The run down the Mexican coast and along the cays and islets of British Honduras is beautiful, with tiny villages white against the forest line and the "Cockscomb" jagged range stretching blue in the distance. From Belize, the capital of the crown colony, it is only a few

GREAT BANANA TREES NEAR QUIRIGUA

These banana trees grow to the height of 40 feet, attaining this growth in a period of 18 months. So rich is the alluvial soil of the plain upon which Quirigua stands that the vegetation here grows at the incredible rate of one-half inch every 24 hours.

A FALLING MONUMENT

These great monoliths, some of which are as much as 26 feet high, were quarried from the foothills two miles west of the city, and were probably transported thither on rafts during the rainy season, when the greater part of the valley is submerged by the overflow of the Motagua River.

Photo by Valdeavellano & Co.

WELL-PRESERVED HIEROGLYPHICS

"Each figure is crowned with a tall feather head-dress; is belted with a short embroidered skirt like the sacrificial apron worn by Korean eunuchs in the Heaven sacrifice—naked, with heavy ornaments at wrist and ankle. On the sides of the stones are columns of glyphs, until now undeciphered, but nearly all plain and well preserved, and, when the clue shall have been found, easily legible."

hours to the Guatemalan border and to the mouth of the Rio Dulce.

This historic waterway (Cortez' road on his superhuman raid from Mexico City to the Honduras coast) opens deep between miles of high wood-hidden cliffs into a vast tide lagoon stretching 30 miles toward the mountains of Vera Paz, "The Land of True Peace" of Las Casas, conquered by him and his Dominican friars when years of fierce fighting had resulted in unvarying disaster and defeat to the Spanish troops at the hands of the warlike Indians.

WHAT THE COAST TOWNS ARE LIKE

Livingston, a Carib town, lies clean and white on a low bluff at the entrance bar, and just opposite, a few miles away by sea, is the real port (Puerto Barrios) more important, but far less sightly, than its neighbor.

Livingston receives the coffee trade from the German plantations of Vera Paz, does a bit of "free trade" on its own account, filibusters and fishes. The soul of the Spanish Main still lives there, and all the game fish of Tampico or Catalina Island are to be found about Puerto Cortez, the next little town, beyond the Motagua River in Honduras, or in the great lagoon above the shady stretches of the Rio Dulce.

Puerto Barrios has a railroad terminal, tank and turn-table, a customs shed, a group of buildings belonging to the United Fruit Company, a barrack for a half company of Carib infantry, and a rotting wooden hotel, all set in a swamp, bridged from house to house by board walks, and made altogether unendurable by mosquitoes. Fortunately one is not obliged to remain in this singularly unattractive place, for the daily train to the capital starts as soon as the passengers are through the customs, and, long before the sun is high, has plunged into a jungle so

thick that a dozen paces from the railroad embankment the sun is invisible.

This dense brush is filled with game: the small deer common to America and Asia, herds of peccary (the small wild pig always cited as a model of fierceness in all the good old books of travel and adventure of our boyhood), tapir, an occasional jaguar, and birds of all kinds, some related to our own game birds.

Monkeys were common enough, but the natives say that they died by the hundred, not a great many years ago, of smallpox. I do not vouch for the diagnosis, but I always visit the jungle with a receptive mind.

A few miles beyond this forest primeval villages begin to line the track, which now follows the Motagua River; groups of huts built of four walls of split bamboo stems set upright in the earth, with a floor of split bamboo laid crosswise and a roof of palm-leaf thatch; some of them are set on the damp and soggy ground and some slightly raised to allow for drainage.

Among these appear others more tidily and securely built of whitewashed plank, inhabited by negroes who come here from the West Indies, Belize, and our own Southern States, attracted by the good pay offered by the fruit company and the railroad. A fair sprinkling of escaped criminals and "bad men" from New Orleans gives to all our American negroes an undeservedly evil reputation on the coast.

THE GREAT BANANA PLANTATIONS

These villages cultivate a little corn, a little fruit, and some gaudy flowers about the huts; but in spite of any attempt at neatness or decoration, they convey only a strong impression of impermanency. Along this part of the river between the bank and a ridge of hills, covered

A MAYA CALENDAR

At the close of each hotun, or 1800-day period, at Quirigua, one of these monuments was erected. The hiero-glyphics carved on the sides probably record the principal events of the corresponding period in each case.

THE CURIOUS EGYPTIAN TYPE

"The faces are well carved, of a heavy, full type, with thick lips, narrow eyes, and thin, carefully pointed Egyptian beards, like the Sargent Pharaoh in the Boston library. Several show a remarkably cruel strength, which lessens with each set of pillars to a weak, purposeless, degenerate type—loose-lipped, chinless, and imbecile" (see text, page 11).

9

TWO INTERESTING FRAGMENTS

The disc to the left shows a figure in profile, which bears a strongly marked resemblance to the types we are familiar with in the ancient Egyptian monuments. This resemblance affords one of the arguments for the theory that this part of America once formed part of a continent called Atlantis, which was peopled by a race closely related to the ancient Egyptians. The figure on the right is a fragment of one of those animal forms which are so common in Maya antiquities.

partly with tropical growth and partly with sickly pines, the banana plantations of the Boston company cover 18,000 acres, mostly developed in the last five years.

In place of the jungle belt, through which I passed on my first visit to Guatemala, are well-ordered sections or "farms" tapped by spur lines of the railway, each fed in its turn by Decauville roads. Each farm is overlooked by the superintendent's house, built like those designed for the Panama Canal workers, well above the ground, with broad porches, screened and mosquito-proof.

The company has of late preferred young college graduates as farm superintendents, and the station name often indicates the founder's school. In the center of all, set in a too-luxuriant rose garden, surrounded by labor villages, shops, storehouses, offices, and "bachelors' quarters," lies the big, comfortable house of the young manager, under whom this extraordinary growth has been attained.

A few miles beyond, 57 from Puerto Barrios and 2½ from the railroad, toward the river, lie the ruins of Quirigua, from the beginning of last year open country like that below, planted with banana "eyes" like a vast potato field, with a lively camp of some 1,800 laborers preparing still more acres.

THE BEAUTIFUL SITUATION OF QUIRIGUA

The ruins lie on low, flat land, flooded and renewed each rainy season by the Motagua's overflow—rich, inexhaustible alluvial soil, and ideal for banana-growing. A more inspiring spot can hardly be imagined. Under the immense ceiba and other coast trees (70 and 80 feet to the lowest branches, each as big as a 30-year maple and hung with orchids or Spanish moss) has grown up a thicket of palms and fern trees, forming, when the underbrush is cleared, arching forest galleries impossible to describe.

From the ceiba and mahogany trees drop long, leafless, snake-like black vine stems—one, the "water-vine," containing a quart of clear, pure water to every foot, which spurts forth in a refreshing stream when cut. It is a real, thirst-quenching water, drawn up from the soil and filtered through the pores of the plant; not a sap, as one might suppose. As is generally the case, this vine grows thickest where the surface water is least drinkable.

Through the arches of the palms suddenly appears a group of mounds, still overgrown with masses of foliage, and beyond these an avenue of great stones, carved monoliths, leading to some—as yet—invisible altar or temple. From each pillar stares—impassive, gloomy, or sullen—a gigantic face. Each figure is crowned with a tall feather head-dress; is belted with a short embroidered skirt like the sacrificial apron worn by Korean eunuchs in the Heaven sacrifice—naked, with heavy ornaments at wrist and ankle.

On the sides of the stones are columns of glyphs, until now undeciphered, but nearly all plain and well preserved, and, when the clue shall have been found, easily legible. The faces are well carved, of a heavy, full type, with thick lips, narrow eyes, and thin, carefully pointed Egyptian beards, like the Sargent Pharaoh in the Boston library. Several show a remarkably cruel strength, which lessens with each set of pillars to a weak, purposeless, degenerate type—loose-lipped, chinless, and imbecile. Among them is to be found the most perfect pieces of carving I have yet seen among American antiquities (see page 9).

CENTERS OF A GREAT CIVILIZATION

It is not to be supposed that either this place or Copán was an isolated group of temples. It is more likely that they were centers, and that more similar, if less perfect, remains will be uncovered in the near future in the course of deforestation preliminary to banana planting.

There is no reason to suppose that the aboriginal dwelling was in any way superior to the bamboo and thatch structures I have described above—than which nothing could well be more perishable. The Motagua Valley and adjacent territory may have been and probably was densely populated about these sacrificial foci; but with the overthrow and savage annihilation of the last of the priest-kings and the flight of their emancipated but terrified subjects to the higher valley of the same river about Gualán and Zacapa, no trace would remain of any but the most substantial buildings, the temples and palaces. "Indian mounds" are frequently reported

THIS MONUMENT, STELA F, IS ONE OF THE MOST BEAUTIFUL
OF ALL THE HOTUN-MARKERS AT QUIRIGUA

It is 25 feet high above ground and is elaborately carved from top to bottom. It records the date 9.16.10.0.0.1
Ahau 3 Zip of Maya chronology, or approximately 490 A. D.

in all this region and have been known for many years to the adventurous spirits who have prospected for gold, railroads, mahogany, game, or "treasure" in these uninhabited forests.

These lie, according to such statements, along the river and in the hills toward the Rio Dulce and the lagoon, with a general trend from Copán to Petén. Some lie in the upper Motagua Valley as far as the foot-hills above Zacapa. The railroad crosses the Motagua a few miles above Quirigua, forced to the right bank by the line of low hills it has followed from the coast.

Almost from the crossing the country begins to change. It becomes less swampy; the river bed grows rocky and no longer flows through deep banks of black earth; it acquires the greenish tinge of mountain streams; and the foliage on the banks, while not less thick, is drier and shows a less feverish green.

Above Gualán (perched picturesquely on a hilltop) the valley opens into a rainless, dusty, cactus-grown plain like northern Mexico or Arizona, surrounded by high bare mountains and watered by two fine rivers—the Motagua still and an affluent, the Zacapa. It is well populated; corn and cotton grow well, and cattle appear to prosper.

Yellow fever, having once got a hold upon this region, has become endemic, but I know of no place whence it might more easily be banished, and, cleaned thoroughly, these towns should be as healthy as any.

The inhabitants are of the "Ladino" class, the Spanish-Indian hybrid, which has, in the course of centuries, become a fixed type. They have a good idea of the possible value of their land, dry and dusty as it is, and will not sell at any price; nor are they in error. Barrage and pumping works installed in the Zacapa River—far beyond the power of native capital, it is true,

but of easy construction for some American syndicate—would make of this plain the richest sugar region in the world. Cane needs heat and unlimited water, but neither wind nor rain. The burning Zacapa plain is sheltered from both, and has an inexhaustible supply of water from the rivers.

A PREHISTORIC MINING CENTER

There is every indication that this region was once as thickly peopled as any part of the country. Records of the missionaries who came after the Spanish conquest tell of large towns here and flourishing villages, and it may be that gold or silver workings gave to the overshadowing range the name it bears, of "Mountains of the Mines." Whether or not this upper valley of the Motagua was peopled from below might still be determined from the relics which remain.

These investigations, however, should be undertaken promptly before the development of all this country by investment of American capital and intensive cultivation has so altered its face that all record is lost. A connection between the upper and the lower Motagua Valley—that is, between the Zacapa Valley and the coast—seems to me to be more logical and natural than a relation between this region and the highlands.

Of the plateau cities destroyed by Alvarado sufficient record is still available to make comparatively easy an exhaustive study of the Quiché, Kakchiquél, and other tribes or nations of the mountains and of the Pacific coast. Rulers and people seem to have been of the same stock, and after their overthrow by the Spaniards and their Tlascalan allies, the survivors did not disappear; they rose again and again

SIDE VIEW OF THE MONUMENT CALLED STELA K

The hieroglyphic inscription shown here records the date 9.18.15.0.0.3 Ahau, 3 Yax of Maya chronology, or approximately 535 A. D. Stela K was the last of the great monuments to be erected at Quirigua, the following hotun, or 5-year period (540 A. D.) being marked by the erection of Temple A.

and fought their conquerors as long as there remained a chief to lead them.

DO THE INDIANS
PRESERVE THEIR TRADITIONS?

The traditions of the ancient people, their religion, and their feeling of nationality may still live in the heart of the Quiché Mountains, and might be easily studied by one who would devote a number of years of his life to acquiring their language and observing their customs and their prejudices, and who would make it his first care to treat them like human beings rather than savages (which, distinctly, they are not), or like beasts of burden. They are not emancipated yet from their martyrdom of centuries; since Bartolomé de las Casas they have had no protector. The republic has done nothing for the Indian, yet they are the finest stock in the country and in them lies the future of Guatemala.

To help him the student will find many treasures in the government archives and valuable historical documents in private collections. Much has found its way out of the country, and it is to be hoped that it is in the hands of some one who will realize the importance to history of these old manuscript books and records and will give it to the world.

The climate during the dry season (on the high plateaus, from October or November to March) is delightful; the high mountain valleys, pine and corn clad, with their soft-toned, well-shaded villages and towns; the true hospitality and gentleness of the people (once one has gained their confidence and affection) make an ideal setting for a winter's work.

The roads are only navigable for bullock-carts, it is true, but a mule or a good native pony will pass anywhere, in spite of bottomless ruts and spring holes. With a good animal, road traveling in Guatemala is, in my experience, unsurpassed for beauty except by the mountain paths of Korea.

There is also a dry season on the coast of which advantage may be taken, and will be taken, I hope, for several years to come, to complete the Quirigua work. When the mud has dried and the ever-vigorous underbrush has been cut from the park surrounding the monuments, a few weeks spent among them is not only not dangerous, but not unpleasant and would certainly be immensely profitable.

EXPLORING, BUT IN TOUCH
WITH CIVILIZATION

As I have attempted to point out, the student is not lost in primeval jungle, but works near a camp which is the center and headquarters of the United Fruit Company's operations. He has but to follow their axemen every morning as they open new territory, and is at all times within easy range of tobacco, clean linen, magazines, good food, and, at the worst, of pills, American doctors, and hospitals.

With the coöperation of the government of Guatemala lies open to the Institute a work of vast importance to American archeology, under conditions—I was about to say—of luxury, and I think that the expression is well justified if comparison be made with any other American work of this character.

Nothing should be spared, in funds or men, to make Mr. Hewett's undertaking a complete success and establish the work in Guatemala upon as permanent a basis as that of San Juan Teotihuacan, in Mexico.

Vol. XXV, No. 6　　　　WASHINGTON　　　　June, 1914

THE HOME OF A FORGOTTEN RACE
Mysterious Chichen Itza, in Yucatan, Mexico

By Edward H. Thompson

Formerly U. S. Consul at Mérida, Yucatan

THE ruined group of Chichen Itza, on the Peninsula of Yucatan, Mexico, covers a space of fully 3 square miles. Over all this wide territory are scattered carved and squared stones in countless thousands, and fallen columns by the hundreds, while the formless remains and outlined walls of huge structures fallen into ruin are seen on every side.

Seven massive structures of carved stone and adamantine mortar still tower erect and almost habitable. Their façades, though gray and haggard with age and seamed by time, sustain the claim that Chichen Itza, in the Americas, is one of the world's greatest monuments of antiquity.

The heart of most of the cities of antiquity was a castle or temple; in this great American monument the heart was a castle and a temple—both in one.

As this is a popular descriptive article rather than a technical one, I shall try to restrain my always present desire and inject only enough figures to give adequate conceptions of size and distance.

A terrace as broad and level as a plain is raised 10 feet or more above the surrounding surface, built up with rubble and finished with a lime cement—hard, white, and durable. On this man-made plain was built, among other structures, a pyramid of nine terraces, each faced with inlaid paneled stonework and well finished.

On each of the four inclined faces of this pyramid a stairway was built 111 feet long and 28.7 feet wide, with 104 steps rising from the base-level up to the crowning platform.

Each of the four angles of the pyramid is formed by the undulating body of a great stone serpent. Descending from the crowning platform, each undulation of the body marks a gradient, a terrace plane, while on each side of the northern stairway a serpent head, with wide-open jaws, carved from a single mass of limestone, rests on the plane beneath. A strong man cannot hope to lift the smallest stone that goes into the making of this serpent body.

THE CASTLE TEMPLE

All this is simply of the base, the preparation for and the leading up to the building proper, the Castle Temple (see page 18). This temple is not large, measured by the standards of the present day, or even by that of those ancient builders. Like the heart of the human body, it was not large but important.

Built on the level platform that crowned the pyramid, it is itself only 43 feet by 29 feet, with a narrow level space around it on the platform's outer edge barely wide enough for two to walk abreast in safety.

On the north, facing a few degrees east of north, is the Ceremonial Stairway, with its two great serpent heads leading up the pyramid to the entrance of the sanctuary.

Thick stone pillars, fashioned always in the conventionalized serpent form, sustain the carved and paneled façade above the entrance to the outer corridor and inner chamber, the sanctuary of the temple. In the semi-gloom of this sanctuary are two square pillars of stone, each supporting massive twin beams of thick sapote wood richly carved. These in their turn help to support the strange triple-vaulted roof of the chamber (see page 19). Sapote wood, like the East Indian teak, is as strong and almost as durable as stone.

Wooden beams, stone pillars, and entrance posts are all carved in low relief (see page 20). Symbols and human figures, some in mask and bearded, and all clothed in ornate regalia, with strange weapons and the flowing plumes of the quetzal, cover their paneled surfaces.

The symbol of the feathered serpent—the body of the rattlesnake, covered with the plumage of the quetzal bird—was to this old civilization what the Cross was to the Christian and the Crescent to the Saracen.

Under this symbol the culture hero *Kukul-can* (Feathered Serpent) of Yucatan, *Quetzacoatl* of the Aztecs and earlier people, was first reverenced, then deified and worshipped.

Most of the carvings on stone surface were painted, but the wooden lintels, carved or plain, were apparently dull finished in their own natural color—a rich red brown.

On the south, east, and west a single high-vaulted but narrow chamber was formed [-shaped, with sapote lintels and carved doorways facing each of the stairways.

Large serpent masks, each flanked by sunken paneled squares, are the only ornaments of these three façades, and, except that on the western façade, are placed directly over the entrances. The mask of this western façade is several feet to the south of the entrance.

This was not a random work, neither did the conformation of the structure make this lack of symmetry a necessary fault.

Is it true that the ancient builders of the East were wont to leave one stone missing or one carving misplaced in an otherwise perfect work because only the Supreme One should produce perfection?

On the roof are ornaments of carved stone cut in curious angles and placed like battlements. These probably served as shelters to the fighting men and protection to the priestly watchers of the stars and planets as they traced the celestial orbits and read the omens thus revealed.

THE GREAT PYRAMID TEMPLE OF CHICHEN ITZA, IN YUCATAN, MEXICO

"On the roof are ornaments of carved stone cut in curious angles and placed like battlements. These probably served as shelters to the fighting men and protection to the priestly watchers of the stars and planets as they traced the celestial orbits and read the omens this revealed" (see text, page 17).

IN THE SEMI-GLOOM OF THIS SANCTUARY ARE TWO SQUARE PILLARS OF STONE,
EACH SUPPORTING MASSIVE TWIN BEAMS OF THICK SAPOTE WOOD, RICHLY CARVED

Sapote wood, like the East Indian teak, is almost as strong and durable as stone. Note the warrior with his elaborate head-dress carved on the column (see page 17).

WOODEN BEAMS AND ENTRANCE POSTS ARE ALL CARVED IN LOW RELIEF

"Wooden beams, stone pillars, and entrance posts are all carved in low relief. Symbols and human figures, some in mask and bearded, and all clothed in ornate regalia, with strange weapons and the flowing plumes of the quetzal, cover their paneled surfaces" (see page 17).

THE SACRED WELL INTO WHICH PRISONERS OF WAR
AND BEAUTIFUL MAIDENS WERE THROWN

Could this deep old limestone water-pit, the sacred well, be given a tongue and made to tell what it has seen, what world romance could equal it!

THE HOUR OF SUNRISE

The writer stood upon the roof of this temple one morning last December just as the first rays of the sun reddened the distant horizon. The morning stillness was profound. The noises of the night had ceased and those of the day were not yet begun. All the sky above and the earth below seemed to be breathlessly waiting for something—just waiting. Then the great round sun came up flaming splendidly, and instantly the whole world sang and hummed. The birds in the trees and the insects on the ground sang in a grand Te Deum.

Nature herself taught primal man to be a sun-worshipper, and man in his heart of hearts still follows the ancient teachings.

A gentle breeze sprang up, and then he seemed to be upon a sea-bound rocky promontory, high above all things. The calm sea surface stretched away to where the sky-line met it, and there they fused into an opalescent something, seemingly born of the union of a rainbow with the white sea-foam.

The sun rose higher and the sea of mist dissolved into nothingness. In its place was an ocean of verdure, with a foam of bright blue flowers, the bloom of the jungle morning glory. As he descended the steps worn by the sandal tread of a thousand years, he thought: "Can this world show a more beautiful sight?"

From the northern edge of the level terrace at the base of the temple pyramid a raised

Photo by Edward H. Thompson

THESE SUPERB WALL SCULPTURES REPRESENT THE PERFORMANCE
OF SOME RELIGIOUS RITE OR CEREMONIAL DANCE

ONE OF THE TWO SMALL TEMPLES WHICH SEEM TO GUARD
THE ENTRANCE TO THE CEREMONIAL COURT (SEE PAGE 26)

THE TEMPLE OF THE TIGERS

The band of handsomely carved jaguars, alternating with shields, can be discerned near the top of the building (see page 26). "Half ruined as it is, the Temple of the Tigers is a treasure and a boon to students of the Maya civilization" (see text, page 28).

causeway, 25 feet wide and macadamized, extends northward 300 yards or more to the Sacred Well.

THE SACRED WELL INTO WHICH PRISONERS AND MAIDENS WERE THROWN

This was the Sacred Way, and in times of pestilence and drought solemn processions of priests, devotees with offerings, and victims for the sacrifice wound between the snake-head columns down the long, steep stairway of the temple and along the Sacred Way to the dreadful Sacred Well (see page 21). The weird music of the flute and the shrill notes of the whistle mingled with the droning boom of the sacred drum as the priests, the devotees with their offerings, and the nobles grouped themselves on the brink of the well.

Then from the platform beside the shrine the offerings from far and near were tossed in, and finally the prisoners of war and beautiful maidens, drugged with the sacred ambrosia Balche, were thrown into the jade-colored waters as expiatory offering to an offended deity.

Could this deep old limestone water-pit, the Sacred Well, be given a tongue and made to tell what it had seen, what world romance could equal it!

Photo by Edward H. Thompson

THE GREAT PARALLEL MOLES OF SOLID MASONRY
WHICH FLANK THE CEREMONIAL COURT

"This level, cemented space was probably the theater for the performance of certain rites and games of a ceremonial character, like the Aztec game dedicated to Tlaloc" (see text, page 26).

Several hundred feet to the west of the Castle Temple, and on the same terrace with it, rest two great parallel moles of solid masonry (see page 25), each 275 feet long, 34 feet wide, and 25 feet high.

Between these moles is the Ceremonial Court. This level cemented space was probably the theater for the performance of certain rites and games of a ceremonial character, like the Aztec game dedicated to Tlaloc.

This belief is borne out by the fact that at a distance of 6 feet from the level upper surface of the mole two great rings of stone were firmly fixed by means of tongues into the perpendicular wall surface directly opposite each other.

One of these rings had either fallen out of its place by its own weight, or more probably was dug out by native honey seekers, and now lies prostrate, but whole, on the ground beneath. The other yet stands out boldly from the sheer wall surface, and the entwined serpents carved on its annular faces are still clearly visible.

To the north and south of these great moles are the half-ruined remains of two small temple structures (see page 23). Shrine-like, they seem to guard the entrance to the Ceremonial Court; but they themselves, their carved walls and columns time worn and beaten, are fully exposed to the wear of the elements.

THE TEMPLE OF THE TIGERS

On the southern end of the eastern mole rests an edifice, like a casket holding jewels, that in time, as the fact becomes known, will be in itself the object of distant pilgrimages.

It is known as the Temple of the Tigers (see page 24) from the zone band of handsomely designed, artistically executed jaguars that, al-

ternating with shields, ornaments the southern face.

Of course, it is understood that the term "tiger" is a misnomer as applied to the great Felidae in America; the jaguar and not the tiger is meant. The term "tigre," meaning tiger, was probably first carelessly given by Spanish adventurers to the jaguar from Asia, and the name was thus wrongly perpetuated in America.

The entire front of the Temple of the Tigers has disappeared. Fractured and wedged apart by the growing tree roots at the apex of the roof, the overweight of the richly carved façade toppled it over into the space beneath, where it still lies in a formless mass.

Two large serpent columns, with open jaws and bulbous teeth, are still in place. These once helped to sustain the fallen façade, and probably served as the massive fulcrum that tossed the mass of stone and lime free from the platform in front down on the level floor of the Ceremonial Court. These, like all the other serpent columns, are carved in the conventionalized crotalid shape and covered with the conventional quetzal plumes.

The square end pilasters of the outer entrance to the inner chamber are entirely covered with sculptures in low relief. Like those upon the pilasters and columns of the Castle Temple, the principal motive on each panel is a human figure elaborately costumed and brilliantly painted.

MAYAN MURAL PAINTINGS

The wall surface of both chambers bear traces of having been once covered with mural paintings. Those on the walls of the outer chamber have become entirely obliterated by the erosive action of the elements. Those on the walls of the inner chamber are in part obliterated by

THE PRISON OR CHICHEN CHOB, PROBABLY THE MOST PERFECT
EXISTING UNIT OF ANCIENT MAYA ARCHITECTURE (SEE PAGE 28)

the excreta of bats, and still more by the vandal hand of man.

Enough yet remains to make this little chamber the repository of the best-preserved examples of the mural paintings of this ancient Maya race at present known.

The best-preserved portion represents a battle scene. The attacking party, with atlatls, spears, and shields, are seemingly assaulting a city or some large center. Above the battlefield can be seen tier upon tier of houses, and amid them are women in agonized postures, looking down upon the fighting warriors.

To one side is the symbolical figure of *Kuk-ul-can*, with lightning-like yellow flames issuing from his mouth, the sign of defiance and

also of war. Many other scenes and portions of figures are depicted, but the battle scene is the clearest of them all at present. The figures are done in a clear, easy style, vigorous and true.

Belonging to this same temple, but on a lower level and built against the eastern wall, is a chamber 22 feet long by 10 feet wide and 15 feet high.

The front of this chamber also is destroyed, and in practically the same way as that of the upper chamber. A portion of the end walls and a large part of the rear still remain upright (see page 22), and the superb wall sculptures they hold upon their surface are fortunately still left for study and comparison.

Clear-cut features, well-worked details, artistically executed and well carried out, show the skill and spirit of these ancient artists. The carvings clearly represent the performance of some religious rite or ceremonial dance. Entwined about the series of masked and conventional figures are the serpent symbol, that of the sun and apparently that of rain and water.

Description is nearly useless in such cases as this; only photographs or drawings can adequately represent the work.

The figures were originally painted in the conventional colors, with the ever-present deep red background.

Portions of the two richly carved square pillars that once helped to sustain the fallen front, and between them a rigid conventionalized "tiger," seemingly a kind of ceremonial seat, complete all that is now visible of this chamber.

Half ruined as it is, the Temple of the Tigers is a treasure and a boon to students of the Maya civilization.

A MAYAN PRISON

South of the Temple of the Tigers lies the beautiful little structure known to the natives as the Chichen Chob, the Prison (see page 27), probably the most perfect existing unit of ancient Maya architecture. The pyramid supporting and the stairway leading up to it are almost intact, the angles and faces of the edifice itself almost perfect.

Within the chambers some of the wooden cross-beams are still in place, the mural paintings on the hard-finished walls are evident, although nearly effaced; but the long band of well-carved hieroglyphics that extend entirely across the wall opposite the doors is as perfect and delicately clear as if carved but yesterday.

To the southeast lies the Round Tower (see page 32), a strange structure, unique in plan and outline. This edifice rises like a turret, 40 feet and of equal diameter, from near the center of a terrace, 20 feet high, 220 feet long by 150 feet wide.

HUMBOLDT'S SURPRISE

Its purpose is at present unknown; but from its construction, annular chambers, winding stairway, and the position of its outlooks and outlets I believe it to have been an observatory, an edifice devoted to the study of the celestial bodies. It is known that the ancient American calendar system was so accurately developed that Alexander Von Humboldt was for a time incredulous of its native origin.

The learned ones, the wise men among these people, were astronomers, not mere stargazers, and there are those among the Mayas at the present day that have a surprising native knowledge of the celestial geography, as well as of curious properties of certain roots and herbs on the earth beneath.

The present conical form of this edifice, the shape of its chambers, and above all the peculiar inner stairway winding around a solid center, have caused the natives to call it, in their vernacular, "The House of the Snail," and this name in its Spanish dress clings to it now. As the *Caracol* (Snail) it is best known to the people of the region, and under this name it is shown to the curious and the visitors from afar.

THE "NUNNERY"

Nearly half a mile to the south of the Castle Temple rises the majestic pile of the "Nunnery" (see page 29). How far this name accurately indicates the original purpose of the edifice is not known; but we do know that among

Photo by Edward H. Thompson

THE MAJESTIC PILE OF THE NUNNERY

"The true beauty of the carvings and the perfect proportions of the structure can never be fitly shown until the debris that now hides the base and destroys the true symmetry of the edifice is removed. . . . The stone lintels over every entrance, existing or blind, built into this face of the end walls are covered with handsome, still legible glyphs. Clearly legible indeed, but as unreadable as a sealed book. Undeciphered and mysterious, they are the pleasure and despair of those who seek to solve the problems that they hold."

these ancient people a certain social organization existed, resembling in a modified form the societies of monks and nuns.

How much or how little of truth is in the name we may not know, but the edifice itself is probably the most ancient of all the structures now standing. How old no one knows; but the fact is evident that the central portion of the structure was old and time worn before the pitted surface and dulled angles were buried in the plastic mass of the newer masonry. Then in time this, too, was hidden under the present walls, new and clear lined then, but now gray and

seamed by time and the elements, and this is a land where the ice never forms, the frost never rises, and dryness is more evident than dampness or moisture.

The façades of these later portions of the great mass of stone and lime are wonderful examples of carved stonework and ancient American symbolism. I doubt if, taken as a whole, their equal exists. The photographic views show this in a measure, and only in a measure.

The true beauty of the carvings and the perfect proportions of the structure can never be fitly shown until the debris that now hides the base and destroys the true symmetry of the edifice is removed. This work should be done by competent direction under supervision of the government.

Two small one-storied edifices, in the nature of detached wings, are on the right and left of the building proper.

One, known as "La Iglesia" Church, is still quite perfect, and the symbolical figures encrusted on its richly worked façade have long been objects of study to the student and of curiosity to the profane.

The other is a still smaller structure of ordinary design and no apparent points of special interest.

A wide, steep stairway, with the very narrow steps and risers common to the work of sandal-wearing people, leads up to the important second story. This portion of the structure sets back from the face of the lower one, thus leaving an open level space of some 30 feet wide, broken in front half way by the stairway leading up to the third story.

The lateral northern face of this upper second story has two true entrances into perfect chambers and four large recesses in the front walls that are either blind doorways or once true entrances into chambers formerly existing in the original structure, but later filled up to make a solid foundation for a third story directly above. When this was done the doorways remained as simple niches, and over these a flying buttress (see page 31) was thrown as a stairway to the newer structure above. This is my hypothesis, subject to modifications that future investigations may make necessary.

The stone lintels over every entrance, existing or blind, built into this face of the end walls are covered with handsome, still legible glyphs. Clearly legible indeed, but as unreadable as a sealed book.

Undeciphered and mysterious, they are the pleasure and despair of those who seek to solve the problems that they hold.

All the chambers within this second story of the edifice have within the wall spaces opposite the entrances various niches about the height of the entrances, but narrower. None, even the smaller chambers, have less than two, and the long, narrow middle chamber on the south face has five.

These may have been doorways, originally giving entrance into the primitive structure, closed when the central portion was made into a solid core; but various circumstances, among them being the presence and position of the recesses in the walls of the end chamber, cause me to throw aside this hypothesis. To me they have all the appearances of having been true niches.

THE RECORDS
OF THIS ANCIENT PEOPLE
WERE DESTROYED BY THE SPANIARDS

They give, in the mind of the student of these old structures, the appearance of having been repositories. Perhaps within these niches were stored the rolls of parchment, the folded books on deerskin and agave paper, the plans and records, and all the written lore of this city of the Maya wise men, the "Itzaes."

Who knows but their contents formed part of that funereal pyre of ancient Maya literature made by the zealot, Bishop de Landa, on the Mani common.

De Landa, seeing on these old rolls of deerskin and volumes of maguey paper signs that he could not read and symbols that he could not understand, concluded that they were cabalistic signs of a diabolical nature, and caused them, together with many other objects of inestimable value to science, to be destroyed by fire on the public square in the Pueblo de Mani.

At that time the old chroniclers tell us there were destroyed 5,000 idols of distinct forms and sizes, 13 altar stones, 22 stones, carved and of small sizes; 27 rolls of ancient hieroglyphics on deerskin, 197 vases of all sizes and patterns, and many other unrecorded objects.

An ancient Spanish chronicler states naïvely that the natives who witnessed the destruction by fire were much afflicted and made a great outcry of woe.

Is it to be wondered that they made a great outcry of woe? They saw not only the sacred

Photo by Edward H. Thompson

OVER THESE A FLYING BUTTRESS WAS THROWN
AS STAIRWAY TO THE NEWER STRUCTURE ABOVE (SEE PAGE 30)

Photo by Edward H. Thompson

THE ROUND TOWER WHICH WAS PROBABLY THE ASTRONOMICAL OBSERVATORY

"From its construction, annular chambers, winding stairway, and the position of its outlooks and outlets I believe it to have been an observatory, an edifice devoted to the study of the celestial bodies. It is known that the ancient American calendar system was so accurately developed that Alexander Von Humboldt was for a time incredulous of its native origin" (see text, page 28).

things calcining in the fervent heat, but also the written lore, accumulated knowledge of their race, going up in smoke and red cinders. Naturally the thinking ones among them "made great outcry."

Around the corners and on the unbroken portions of the smooth, hard finish in the recesses are traces of broad red, blue, and green bands forming the paneled outlines for the detail figures within. On the ceiling in places are still the fragmentary outlines of houses, trees, city walls, and nondescript animals.

On the inner walls of the eastern end chamber can be clearly seen the impress of the "red hand," another of the unsolved problems.

The third upper story is small and presents the idea of incompleteness, although its state of ruin prevents the last word being said until excavation and investigation have taken place under some competent person.

The last and least important of the seven structures yet standing is the so-called "House of the Dark Writings." The structure is a huge one-story edifice. Large forest trees grow over its flat roof, and were it not for its vertical wall faces of well-carved stone one could easily believe that he was treading the primeval forest floor.

The name, *Akab tzib*, House of the Dark Writing, was given to it by the natives because in the gloom of an inner chamber can be seen a lintel of stone, covered with glyphs and having on its under surface a seated figure in the act, apparently, of offering up some kind of burnt sacrifice.

This ends the list of the still existing structures; but the wonders to be seen prostrate and those hidden have not yet been mentioned.

We have not mentioned the sepulchers of the high priests, 90 feet beneath the crown of the pyramid, 50 feet in the solid rock; the rock carvings; jaguars carved on the ledge surface; the great natural well from whence this ancient city received its water supply; the caves, with their prehistoric defenses, stalactites, grottoes, and pools of clear, cool water—these and many other things we have the desire to depict and describe, but time and space forbid.

WHEN WAS THIS CITY FOUNDED?

How old is this great city of stone-built temples and myriad carvings? For years we have sought among its fallen columns and toppled walls for that which would tell us clearly of its age.

To a certain extent the search has not been in vain. We have found a tablet of stone covered with hieroglyphs, and among them are signs that fix a date, an epoch. Keen minds and trained are now at work on the tablet, and the time may not be far distant when we shall know whether it be 2,000 years old or less, as some students claim, or over 11,500 years, as claimed by Le Plongeon.

The margin between the two "guesses" is certainly wide enough.

Meanwhile, like the Sphynx in the East, the gray, old human faces carved high on the massive walls gaze down unchangingly, unmindful of modern man and his futile guesses.

We have perhaps more information on the early history of this ancient group than we have of any other center of the Maya civilization.

But as that keen scholar, the lamented Dr. Thompson, was fond of impressing upon his pupils, "Gentlemen, information may or may not be facts, and unless it be of proven facts is not knowledge." Even "information" concerning these ancient builders and their buildings is only too scanty, and actual proven facts still more so.

THE LEGEND OF CHICHEN ITZA

The earliest information concerning Chichen Itza is given in a curious document found by Don Juan Pio Perez, a Yucatan scholar and antiquarian, among the dusty old records and archives in the Town Hall of Mani.

The document commences thus: "Lai u tzolan katun lukci ti cab ti yotoch Nonoual"— I might continue on in this way for some time, but all might not understand the text as clearly as could be wished. In fact, the fear of a sudden rupture of relations between writer and reader induces me to forego, and in place give a broad interpretation of the ancient writings in those parts where allusion is made to Chichen Itza.

Translated, the document commences thus, the brackets being my interpolations:

"This is the series of epochs that elapsed from the time of their departure from the house of Nonoual in the land of Tulapan.

"Then took place the discovery of Bacalar. Sixty years they ruled in Bacalar, when they came here.

"During these years of their government of this province of Bacalar occurred the discovery of Chichen Itza. 120 years they ruled in Chichen Itza, when they left it and went to Champutun, where the Itzaes, holy men, had houses.

"260 years reigned the Itzaes in Champutun, when they abandoned it and returned in search of their homes.

"For several epochs they lived in the woods and the caves, under the uninhabited hills.

"After forty years they returned to their homes (Chichen Itza) once more, and Champutun knew them no more.

"Two hundred years they reigned in Uxmal, Chichen Itza, Mayapan. The governor of Chichen Itza (Chac xib chac) was deposed because he murmured disrespectfully against Tunac-eel, the governor of Mayapan. Ninety years had elapsed, but the tenth of the 8th Ahau was the year in which he was overthrown."

The unknown native writer keeps on; but I will stop, as he mentions Chichen Itza no more.

Neither the name nor the history of its writer is known; but from the perfect command of both the native vernacular and the Spanish letters it would seem to have been the work of an educated native and written within a few decades after the conquest. This would not be strange, for many bright young natives, sons of the nobles and of the reigning families, were taken by the church or by high lay officials and educated in Spanish learning.

Thus Caspar Antonio Xiu, the lineal descendant of the last king of Mayapan, was taken, baptized, and educated by Montejo, the conqueror of Yucatan and its first governor.

THE ANCIENT MAYAS HAD THEIR BARDS AND STORY-TELLERS

The ancient Mayas, like most other races, had their bards and story-tellers, who interwove into their songs and tales the history of their people.

Thus, I repeat, it is not strange if some educated native filled, like the gifted Tescucan Ixtlilxochitl, prince and writer, with the desire to perpetuate the fading history of his people, had recourse to the device of writing out, as his memory served, their early wanderings and ancient history, and then, with native subtlety, to hide the documents under those longest filed away and in archives likely to be safe and undisturbed until times far later.

There is a legend of Chichen Itza that has seemingly more of the material of true history in its making than legends are usually thought to have. At all events, it is genuinely romantic and worth repeating.

THE LEGEND OF CANEK

Canek, the impetuous young ruler of Chichen Itza, was deeply in love with a beautiful maiden, daughter of the ruler of a distant province. No longer were his thoughts on the coming hunt of the jaguar; the wild boar passed grunting and unharmed, even unnoticed, as the young ruler sat musing on a fallen log. A fawn, chased by the hunters, became entangled in a snare close beside him as he sat motionless, happily musing. Seeing that its big, soft eyes were like those of the maiden he loved, he loosed its bonds and set it free.

In the midst of his amorous musings, as he sat in his chamber one day, a dust-covered run-

Photo by Edward H. Thompson

A PAGE OF STONE THAT NO MAN MAY YET READ

"How old is this great city of stone-built temples and myriad carvings? For years we have sought among its fallen columns and toppled walls for that which would tell us clearly of its age. To a certain extent the search has not been in vain. We have found a tablet of stone covered with hieroglyphs, and among them are signs that fix a date, an epoch. Keen minds and trained are now at work on the tablet, and the time may not be far distant when we shall know whether it be 2,000 years old or less, as some students claim, or over 11,500 years, as claimed by Le Plongeon" (see text, page 33).

ner came up to the palace entrance and rattled the sounding shells before the curtains for instant entrance on the ruler's service.

The news he brought drove the young ruler to desperation.

The Batab of a neighboring province, and one far more powerful than he of Chichen Itza, had married the maiden that Canek was to take to wife.

For a while no raging jaguar robbed of his mate was more furious than young Canek; then of a sudden he grew quiet, cool, and seemingly calm.

So his warriors remembered to have seen him when they fought an old-time enemy, killed his fighting men, and defaced his temple, and they patiently waited.

The night came and with it a brooding norther. Darkness as black as the hate in the heart of Canek was all around the silent ranks of the swiftly moving warriors. The lightning flashes, as sharp and hot as the anger that flamed in the Canek's breast, played over the glinting points of crystal on the moving forest of lances as they neared the enemy's city.

The ever-burning flames on the top of the distant temple gleamed redly, and black smoke went heavenward in increasing volume as the priests burnt great baskets of copal in honor of their ruler's marriage.

Canek and his silent warriors came swiftly onward, melting into the darkness of the shadows, hiding from the lightning flash, leaping ahead like deer when chance offered. Revelry had taken the city with all that was in it and held it hard and fast. Even the watchers were drunkenly grumbling over the fate that kept them out of the carousals and in the darkness. As the black and moving shadows reached them swiftly they soon were quiet and out of the darkness for evermore.

THE INTERRUPTED MARRIAGE

And the deer-eyed woman—a wife, yet still a maiden—was she happy? Oh, who knows! It may be that her eyes were not pain shadowed; that it was but the dim light of the wild wax tapers in the narrow vaulted chamber, and it may be that which glistened on her drooping lashes was but the flashing of stray light beams from between the entrance curtains. Who knows?

Merry were the wedding guests and well drunken most of them. More than merry was the bridegroom, who drank the deepest of them all. His brain was sodden, his limbs rebellious, but his tongue, though thick and clumsy, still responded to his call.

Sodden brain and clumsy tongue worked together as he mumbled loudly:

"As for the Lord of Chichen Itza—poor lean dog—let him take his pleasure howling at the moon tonight! Before I seek my wife's caresses in her many-curtained chamber, I must hear a lively song. Ehen! Holcanes! Tupiles! lift your voices and rattle out the battle song."

Drunkenly mumbling, stupidly fumbling, he rolled on his side and fell asleep.

At the holcanes' call the tupiles started the great war song of the Mayas—"Conex, Conex Paleche" ("Come on, come on, ye warriors").

The voices that commenced it were well known, though drunken and quavering; the voices that joined in it and ended it were strong, full, and shrilly menacing. Abruptly the drunken voices ceased and some ended with a groan.

The deer-eyed woman, alone in her curtained chamber, heard the voices and the singing, and then the strangeness of the tumult drove her to the carved stone entrance. Before she reached it the shells were rattled and the curtains parted swiftly. "Star of the night! Star of my life!" said Canek.

"My Lord Canek," said the maiden, with startled eyes, but star lit.

Dead men, live men, and the live men dead in drunken stupor, what could the few with senses unbenumbed do against the silent fury of Canek and his fighting men?

Never again did Chichen Itza know its Lord Canek, nor any of his band of fighting men. In the passing of a night they vanished, the Lord Canek and the soft-eyed maiden, the stolen bride of the drunken one.

Time passed. The lord who won a bride, but did not learn to keep her, lived his life, died, and was forgotten.

The memory of Lord Canek lived on in song and story and became a part of the legends of Chichen Itza.

THE LOST IS FOUND

One day, long after, a hunting band from Chichen Itza went toward the south—some days' journey. Young men they were and full of rashness, so they kept on the chase until the land grew hilly and higher, and at last rose into the very clouds. Wonderingly, they turned homeward, journeying over a strange country, until they reached a lake of shining water, and in the lake an island city, with houses and temples and the carved fronts of many buildings like their own Chichen Itza.

From this island city warriors came and met them and led them to the waiting ruler and his aged wise men.

"Who are you, presumptuous ones, that you dare to come unbidden on our land and un-

wanted to our city?" asked the Batab in stern menace.

The young man spoke bravely, coolly: "We came from our home, Chichen Itza, and have wandered here unbidden because in the chasing of the deer we went farther than we knew; and, finding pathways right before us, we kept on, thinking to find old friends or make new ones."

The ruler turned and took counsel with his wise men, then said to the waiting hunters: "If your tale be true, that you are of Chichen Itza *and not of another province*, you will indeed find here old friends new made—old friends and new as well.

"This is the city of Tayasal, whose lord is Canek, who once was lord of your own Chichen Itza, the City of the Sacred Well."

This is the legend. The substance is as told by the good old, but very dry, chronicler, Padre Cogolucco. I confess to have taken this skeleton and put a little flesh on here and there, just to round out the form—a little brown and red, just to give a local coloring, and so produce the true general effect; that is all. But perhaps I had better have left it as the ancient priestly scribe tells it; "quien sabe"—who knows?

Not all of the tales of Chichen Itza are prehistoric or legendary.

Far later, chronologically, than the legend of Canek, a proven fact, with only a small portion of "information" embedded in it, is furnished us, and brings us down to the historic times of the early Spanish conquerors, when they were in deadly struggle with the fearless Mayas.

MONTEJO WELCOMED

In 1525-1526 Montejo was weary with his long and seemingly fruitless struggles

Photo by Edward H. Thompson

PHOTOGRAPH OF A HUMAN HEAD CARVED IN STONE: PORTION OF A RICHLY CARVED
WALL SURFACE RECENTLY DISCOVERED AT CHICHEN ITZA

All the rolls of parchment and books on deerskin and agave paper, all the plans and records and the written
lore of the mysterious city, Chichen Itza, were burned by the Spanish zealot, Bishop de Landa. When he saw
the Maya symbols that he could not understand, he concluded that they were signs of a diabolical nature and
caused them, together with many other objects containing Maya records, to be destroyed by fire on the public
square of the city (see page 31).

against the native Mayas. Constantly buffeted by his countless enemies and having no place of refuge, he found himself in imminent danger.

The overlords of the provinces near the coast, known by the name of *Cheles* (bluebirds), were in a way friendly to the Spaniards, and Montejo found his way toward them. The other Indians, seeing that the Spaniards were headed coastward and thinking that they were seeking to return from whence they came, did not seek to fight or in any way annoy them; thus the Spaniards arrived safely at the home of the *Batabs Cheles.*

These received them hospitably and, in response to the petition of Montejo, allowed them to find a safe asylum at Chichen Itza, then governed by a vassal chief, Cupul.

Upon their arrival, Cupul, according to a native document, "The Narrative of Nahum Peck," said to them:

"Stranger lords, take your rest in these halls," and they did; they made themselves very much at home, after the manner of the Spanish conquerors of those days, even before they had fairly earned the proud title.

For a time the Indians bore the burdens that their guests put upon them with meekness, but at last they rebelled at having to be the providers and burden-bearers for such lusty feeders and poor paymasters, and then their actions soon put the Spaniards in a serious plight.

Finally, besieged and almost without provisions, they took advantage of a stormy night after a brave sortie to deceive the Indians. One by one they deserted the edifice used as their garrison and stole away in the darkness, to unite and make for a more friendly haven.

DOG, ROPE, AND BELL

It is said that to deceive the Mayas into thinking that they were there they tied a dog to the rope of a bell and placed food in front, just beyond his reach. His frantic efforts to get at the food rang the bell at frequent intervals, while the constant bark aided the supposed deception of the Mayas, and when at last the ruse was discovered the little band of Spanish soldiery was nearly out of the enemy's reach.

Thus runs the chronicle, and the story may be true; but, knowing, as the writer does, the character and customs of the direct descendants of these same old Maya warriors, he does not believe it. It is far more probable that these Mayas, desiring to be quickly and peacefully rid of their burdensome guests, shut their eyes to the going of the Spaniards and would have been the more obliged to them if they had taken the bell and the dog along with them as well, and so left the besiegers to enjoy their early slumbers undisturbed. The discreetly dropped eyelid, that is almost a wink, and quickly changes into a blindness, is an artful act as ancient as the human race. In many respects the logic of the native Maya is peculiarly his own, but in many other ways his acts and artifices are as old as man himself.

ELOQUENT SILENCE

The writer has often been asked, "After one has visited the ruins of the Old World, is it worth while to visit those of the New World?"

He has had as visiting guests scientists of other lands, men with the wonders of Italy, of Egypt, and India fresh in their memory, inquisitive, incredulous, but desiring to see what there was to see.

As these great, lonely monuments loomed up before their vision, he has noted the quick, surprised intake of the breath, the change of color even, and then—a speaking silence far more eloquent than any words could be.

The American people should awaken to the fact that they have right at home, at their very doors, architecture essentially American, as it were, ruined structures every whit as interesting, as massive, and possibly as old as those of other lands, whose boast it is that the Americans must come to them, for "America has no ruins."

Within these mysterious ruins—American ruins—are great books, with pages of stone, writ in characters that no man may yet read. Are the mysteries they hold, the wonderful facts, that certainly lie sealed and mute within them, hidden from us, less interesting to Americans than are the tales of Egyptian dynasties, the rites of Druids, Roman campings, or Saxon raidings? I think not.

THE VENICE OF MEXICO

By Walter Hough

ONE of the pleasurable experiences among those that delight the traveler in Mexico is a visit to the home of the Aztec lake dwellers. Much of the charm of the great Valley of Mexico, where they live, is due to the stretches of water among the trees and verdant fields in a landscape framed in beautiful mountains and bathed with clearest air of heaven.

Their lakes—Texcoco, Xochimilco, Zumpango, and Chalco—do not reveal themselves except from the high mountains encircling the valley. They are shallow bodies of water in the midst of extensive marshes, unapproachable, and lacking the effect of our lakes with their definite shore-lines. For this reason, they have never been highways of civilized commerce, nor has navigation flourished in their shallow waters; but they were from these very hindrances destined to be jealous mothers of ancient and remarkable States, whose people, protected in the fens, dug out canals and developed an indigenous commerce and transportation to the fullest extent.

DRAINING THE LAKES OF THE VALLEY OF MEXICO

They were for modern man a constant menace during seasons of flood and have required enormous engineering works to keep them in bounds. The first of these, never of great value, was begun some 300 years ago, and exists at the present time as a gigantic ditch over 13 miles long, 197 feet deep, and 361 feet wide, dug by the patient labor of impressed Indians, and called the Tajo de Nochistongo. The latest undertaking is a canal connecting the three lakes and leading their waters out of the valley by a tunnel through the eastern mountains. This splendid piece of engineering, completed some years ago, effectually controls the height of the water in the lakes and prevents inundations.

But long before Cortez came the Indians of the valley worked in the boggy lake lands and dug canals hither and thither—main canals between the lakes and to the great city of Tenochtitlan and smaller canals between their fields. Through this maze of waterways, then as now, they sent their boats and in the fens built their

NAVIGATION ON THE CANAL IN MEXICO CITY

Once the wealth and beauty of Mexico dwelt along the boulevard bordering the National Canal; but its glory is departed, and a tawdry, odoriferous, peon-infested neighborhood it has become. When the annual flower festival at the little village of Santa Anita takes place, however, it becomes alive with color, and riotous good humor prevails.

IN THE VALLEY OF MEXICO

The Valley of Mexico is a semi-arid plateau, a mile and a half higher than Washington, D. C., and is surrounded in turn by high mountains, with only a few natural passages. Its greatest length is 71 miles and its greatest width 45 miles, although its average length is less than 50 miles and its average width less than 40. When the mountains which surround the valley were thrown up by volcanic cataclysms, they are supposed to have inclosed the valley entirely. During ages that followed the valley was a large lake, with numerous islands dotting its surface. In the day of the Aztecs the water had subsided, leaving many small lakes instead of the one large one. The coming of the Spaniard resulted in the cutting of a drainage canal through the mountain and the disappearance of most of these lakes.

thatched houses. Historically, Cortez was the first European boat-builder in the New World, when of an imperious necessity he launched his brigantines, of quaint sixteenth century pattern, if one may believe the artists, in the reeking waters of Tezcoco at the spot near Huejutla, where there is now a bridge called Puente de los Bergantines, not far from the capital.

Pere Sahagun, the Franciscan, records that "the City of Mexico is like another Venice, and the people themselves are comparable to the Venetians in urbanity and savoir." This was written in the sixteenth century, but in the lapse of several hundred years the city's wonderful water environment has become dry ground, and the seeker for lake dwellers will have to look farther afield in the entrancing valley of the sky.

The way to the present Aztec Venice, which bears the name of Xochimilco, "in the field of flowers," is through one of these ancient canals—a prehistoric water road from Tenochtitlan to the capital and seat of one of the group of seven Aztec tribes which long ago came from remote Aztlan to the rich Valley of Mexico.

LAKE XOCHIMILCO IN THE ENVIRONS OF MEXICO CITY

The lakes of the Valley of Mexico are noted for their beauty, and not the least of them is Xochimilco, which is connected with the capital by the Canal de la Viga.

A MEXICAN WATER WAGON

In Mexico City one can see almost every form of land transportation that civilization has to offer. Here is the peon with a load on his back. There one sees a sled used before wheels were invented, and across the way a solid-wheeled wagon of a design antedating the invention of spokes. Here is a carriage, there a street-car, and farther up the street a modern automobile carrying passengers to a railroad train about to start out of the city. Now and then a flying machine tries out its wings, and the gamut from the human burden-bearer to the most modern carrier is run.

HARD TO GET A START

The life on the canal, vivid and pictur-esque, is as striking now as it was then; it may even be suspected that the change from that time to this has not been very great. It is hard to get a start to the land of the fens in more ways than one—the negotiations for passage in a barge with boatmen who display the charac-teristics of that tribe known the world over; and the conflicting claims also of all the costumes, incidents, shipping, and so forth, of the boil-ing, squirming kaleidoscopic canal and shore population on its multifarious quests bewilder the beholder and make him forget that he is on a journey to see the lake dwellers in their primi-tive homes. Tardily, then, the barga comes into the clear pool in front of the medieval toll-gate fortress, where all shipping must go under a low bridge and where the old-time toll collector, armed with a pike, could threaten the recalci-trant without much effort.

Beyond the gateway begin more vistas of a new world! On this canal, bordered with trees and spanned by quaint bridges, is a perfect

INDIANS BOATING ON ONE OF THE CANALS IN THE VALLEY OF MEXICO

If these Indians were to live "the sanitary life" as thoroughly as they do "the simple life," there would prob-ably be more centenarians in Mexico than in any other country.

LAKE PATZCUARO: MEXICO

The people who live along the shores and on the islands of Lake Patzcuaro live much to themselves, mingling with the outer world only when absolutely necessary. They use primitive log dugouts and make their living by fishing and hunting wild fowl. They are very fond of a species of salamander, the axolotl, commonly known to many as the water lizard. It has bushy external gills, similar to those which permanently characterize the mud puppy; its color is a mixed black and white. The flesh resembles that of the eel.

stream of craft, from the slender dugout *cha-loupe* to the square-bowed flat-boat, hurrying on with everything to feed, repair, and adorn the great city. Freight is of all descriptions, but one looks curiously on the small bundles of grass and other green forage for animal feed, the pulque barrels, vegetables, and flowers.

The Indian boatmen, clad in white cotton shirt and trousers, are working with a will, sometimes wading in the canal and drawing the heavy-laden boats after them; and alas! returning to their paradise, a woman piloting her husband who is the worse for pulque.

LIFE IN LAKE-LAND

There are pictures and pictures innumerable, full of human interest and checkered with a marvelous play of light, shadow, and reflection, as we pass by the gardens and openings of the larger and smaller canals. Here are embarkings and arrivals loading, unloading, and preparing to lay by for the night in a snug slip near where thatched houses play hide and seek in the luxuriant foliage; here a group of energetic washerwomen by the water margin, and there clouds of white or gaudy, much-belabored clothes on the bushes. No secrets are here; all goes on with the pulsing, urging force of labor freely and openly before men.

One remembers gardeners and gardens in the sunny flower and vegetable plots and children peeping out on the canal highway from under umbrageous trees. Flotsam and jetsam in the canal are vagrant bulbs and flowers of water hyacinth, a wicked, beautiful plant, whose reproductivity makes men work to keep it down, but here it has met its match and is made to be useful. Bridges there are, and most quaint, like that perfect arch of Ixticalco, under which white geese seem to float in the air.

One feels that this panorama should last forever, especially if he does not have to supply the labor of locomotion. Here at this landing at Xochimilco it must be realized that the mere first leaves of our experience, the loveliness of the country of the lake dwellers, are just unfolding.

HIDDEN BEAUTIES OF XOCHIMILCO

The town is really built on terra firma, as the seven churches, each well supplied with raucous bells, the streets of quaint houses, and the broad lava-paved prehistoric market-place, well attest; but the town disguises and hides away the life of the canals and gardens, and its attractions for the tourist are soon compassed.

Photograph by Harriet Chalmers Adams

AN AQUEDUCT THAT HAS STOOD SINCE THE DAYS OF THE CONQUISTADORES

Labor was cheap, even according to the Mexican standard, in the days of the Conquistadores, and the aqueducts that were built then were so well constructed that in many places they are still in perfect condition.

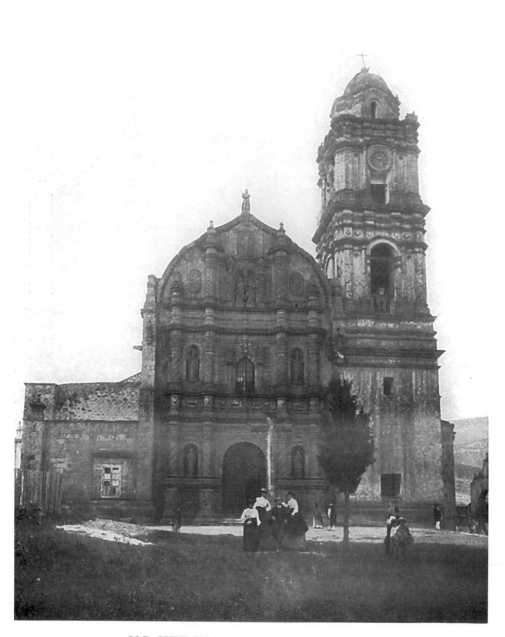

OLD CHURCH AT TLALPUJAHUA, MEXICO

Tlalpujahua is in the region inhabited by the Tarascan Indians, which lies due west of Mexico City. According to Prescott, the Tarascans had a Noah, called Trezpi, who escaped from a great flood in a boat laden with animals. Instead of a dove, Trezpi sent out a vulture first, and then a humming-bird, according to the legend. The methods of courtship in vogue among the Tarascans are peculiar. The lover goes to the spring where the object of his affection is accustomed to fill her water-jar. He holds her shawl until she accepts him, and then, with a stick, he breaks the jar which she holds on her head and gives her a betrothal baptism of water. These Indians once possessed the secret of tempering copper, an art now lost to the world.

THE COLLEGIATE CHURCH,
WITH THE CHAPEL ON THE HILL IN THE BACKGROUND

This is the holiest shrine in Mexico. It stands on the site where the Virgin is reputed to have appeared to an Indian, Juan Diego, instructing him to take a message to the archbishop asking that a shrine be built there in her honor. After appearing to him several times, she finally commanded him to climb to the top of the hill, where the chapel now stands, but which had always been barren, and there to gather a bunch of roses to take to the archbishop. This he did; but when he unfolded his serape it was found to contain, so the account runs, a miraculously painted picture of the Virgin. This picture is now venerated by all Mexicans and occupies the center of the altar. The features and complexion are those of an Indian princess.

We turn into a narrow lane leading away from the formal streets and emerge into an Indian dooryard, and within a few feet of us is the main canal with its boats and floating water plants. The inhabitants of this little house group into which we have come as from another sphere are interested and friendly and ready to visit.

José, the active leader of the family, is going to take us to see the sights of the lake, and soon we are darting along other water streets bordered with spire-like willows, turning the corners and passing impressionistic gardens of cabbages, lettuce, pinks, and roses, until all sense of direction is lost. Soon the waterscapes become more extensive, and the barelegged Aztec boatmen bring up over Los Ojos, the springs, which they call the source of the lake, and hold in a veneration inculcated by ancient lore and customs. Really, the spot is most impressive.

WATER-SELLERS AND THEIR DONKEYS ON THE SHORES OF LAKE CHAPALA

It is hard to realize, in a country where tap-water is universal in urban communities and well and springs everywhere in rural regions, what it means to live where you have to buy it at so much per jarful; and yet millions of Mexicans get their water via the "mule-back" route.

A VINE BRIDGE SPANNING A MEXICAN RIVER

In the art of making use of things provided by Nature-at-hand rather than by Industry-at-a-distance, the Mexican is something of a genius. He can build a bridge with no other tool than a machete, a wagon without a nail or a screw, and a house without a piece of iron in its construction. He does not need to go back to Nature—he has always been there.

When the Xochimilcans, in the days of their idolatry, worshiped their lacustrian spring, they placed therein a black stone image on the sparkling sand bottom of the crater-like fountain, where it was surrounded with plumy water plants, and to this deity offerings of copal, pottery, and other effects were made.

IDOLS AND SKULLS IN SPRING

Sahagun relates the sincere pleasure which he felt when he accomplished the raising of the god of the fountain from his mossy bed and substituted in the place a stone cross. This holy object can no longer be seen; but the litter of broken pottery now there is not ancient, and one suspects that the *costumbre* of oblations may have come down to modern times.

Several bleached skulls of horses were also seen in the spring—why no one can tell; but probably there is a folk belief or a horse worship begun with those war steeds of Cortez, to account for it. The springs have come out of their mystery in recent years and have been prosaically made to supply purer water to the City of Mexico.

These springs, as one sees them now, are bowls 100 feet in diameter and 30 to 40 feet deep, with water clear as crystal and cold, bursting up in the lake at the foot of the Sierra de Ajusco and fed by the snows. It is a remarkable experience to lunch there and drink the good water to the health of the spirit of the springs who has a choice assortment of broken crockery in his keeping. Views of snowy

© Underwood & Underwood

THE WIVES AND CHILDREN OF THE MEXICAN SOLDIERS FOLLOWING THEM ABOUT

There is always to be found near a Mexican encampment a section where the wives and children live. In many of the Mexican battles women have taken part. This picture shows the women and children on the roof of one of the troop trains.

Popocatepetl are glimpsed up the vistas of the lanes between the floating gardens on the return and heighten the lovely reflections of the evening.

The houses of the amiable Xochimilcos are flimsy structures, but well-built and neat, and a visitor receives quite a favorable impression of the people. The pretty children make friends

Photograph by Frank H. Probert

OFFERING DRAWN-WORK FOR SALE TO TOURISTS ON A MEXICAN RAILROAD

The Mexican Indian woman seems to have been born with a needle in her hand. Her drawn-work, for delicacy, beauty, and grace of design, is surpassed by none in the world. She can take the sheerest of handkerchief linen and draw out threads in a way that is the admiration and despair of many a cultured needlewoman.

Photograph by Capt. D. H. Scott, U. S. A.

A PAIR OF MEXICAN SUSPECTS

These sheep may be camp pets, but their days of preferment depend largely upon the ability of the commissary department to supply other stewing ingredients. The training of burros and sheep as pets serves to break the monotony of camp life during periods of inaction in Mexico. Hours are spent and patience tested while off duty in trying to teach young lambs old tricks.

easily and load down the Americano with presents of flowers loved by the lake dwellers as they were by their Aztec ancestors. Any one who shows a liking for flowers has won the way to their affection.

In the slip of the canal are the boats owned by the Indians living in the little group of three or four houses belonging to our friends, who combine the vocations of boatmen, gardeners, and fishermen, the latter plying huge nets that seem oversized for the tiny quarry inhabiting the desolate lakes. The gardener works with the primitive tools of his ancestors, and the boatman takes extravagant pride in his dugout *chaloupe*, which is his ancient water vehicle, and also prizes his passenger canoe and freight barge, if his family is rich enough to own them.

© Underwood & Underwood

U. S. INFANTRY AT THE END OF A SIX-DAY HIKE IN MEXICO

A nation could not find a more inhospitable region in which to campaign than northern Mexico. Desolate, barren, the land sterile, the people poor, the landscape depressing in its somber monotony, there is little to lighten the heart or to lift a weight from the soul. Woe is written in the faces of its people and despair upon the face of the land.

GARDENS BUILT
ON HYACINTH FOUNDATIONS

Without moving from José's dooryard, we may by good fortune see a neighbor constructing a "floating" garden, and we are carried back without effort several centuries into the past. From the canals the busy Aztecs throw great masses of water hyacinth upon the strip of bog to the thickness of a foot or more. The water hyacinth, which unfortunately does not fit into the ancient picture, is provided with large cellular floats—a natural provision for its dissemination, which has made it an obstruction to navigation in some of our southern rivers.

Upon this bed of floats they spread a layer of muck, dredged from the bottom of the canals. Perhaps before the plant floats have decayed, these gardens may drift away should the water rise. Even now on portions of the lake square miles of vegetation cover the surface like the "sudd" of the Nile, and the canal roads have to be staked at the sides to keep them from disappearing. Great drifts of microscopic vegetation cover the stagnant water of the open lakes with a mantle lovely in color, while the bottom is coral red from a weed that thrives in the water.

The term "floating gardens" was properly applied by the early historians of Mexico to masses of water weeds covered with a layer of rushes bearing a thin layer of soil, employed by the Mexicans at a period when the fluctuating waters of the lakes prevented the formation of permanent *chinampas*, and so in the New World the Indians repeated the famed gardens of the lakes of Cashmere.

FLOATING GARDENS
REQUIRE IRRIGATION

From the abundance at José's and on every side it is evident that the Xochimilcans are expert gardeners and assiduous at their work. Most of their plants are started in seed beds, from which they are transplanted to the *chinampas*, and it is strange to see boat loads of corn sprouts brought to be planted in this manner. Curiously enough, these morass gardens sometimes require irrigation, which is accomplished by throwing on water from the canal with a wooden scoop.

While we sit in these peaceful surroundings, we cannot but reflect that in some ways it is hard to convince the ordinary observer that the modern is the ancient, and make him realize how much the life of this lake village is a vivid rendering of that of the prehistoric lake dwelling, whose cycle extended from the rude Stone Age through the Bronze Age to the Iron Age, and whose lost and castoff objects sunk in the mud, form now a wondrous museum filled with the history of their progress—the romance of art, wars, and love otherwise unchronicled in an era when letters were not known. So the story was repeated in Florida, in Venezuela, in Ireland, in the Vale of Cashmere, in the East Indies, and in various parts of the world where tribes lived over the water for protection.

The Xochimilcos settled in prehistoric times at a place now called the South of the Valley, and later they extended their villages to the southern slope of Popocatepetl and along the mountains that connect the great volcano with the Sierra de Ajusco, which overhangs the lovely valley of Mexico.

MAKING UNFRIENDLY NATURE
A SERVANT

It is said that when the Aztecs came to Anahuac they were not strong in number and were compelled to inhabit the morasses, because they had not power to dispossess the settled populations which had occupied the favored locations. In this seemingly inhospitable but, as we have seen, protecting and stimulating environment, the Aztecs gradually increased in population and culture and became powerful enough to sweep away the ancient civilizations that occupied the valley and make themselves masters of their heritage.

These movements had been accomplished when Cortez came on the scene. The vast floods, which were very destructive to the towns situated on land lying little distance above the water level, did not much incommode the hardy lake dwellers, whose gardens would float, if necessary, riding moored to stakes, until the waters fell.

The visitor to the homes of the Xochimilcos may thus reconstruct history that is replete with interest. He will see, as Cortez saw, a people lighter in color than any North American Indians, below medium stature, with muscular and well-knit bodies commendably clean through daily ablutions.

SORROW AT BIRTH; JOY AT DEATH

It cannot be said that the Xochimilcan man has an open and ingenuous countenance, but it shows force of character and lights up quickly in response to kindness and recognition. The young women have round, often ruddy, but rather expressionless faces; the children are

pretty, and the older women are better preserved than the women of the Pueblos of the
southwestern United States. Both sexes work
hard, and where there is such uniformity of poverty the struggle for existence makes life a serious matter and engraves deep lines in the faces
of the breadwinners.

Thus a birth is heralded with mourning and
a death with rejoicing. Their music is monoto-
nous and disagreeable to the educated ear, and
their amusements seem to be few; but, given ad-
vantages, these people show skill in the arts, and
as musicians they have made the Mexican bands
known all over the world. They are gifted, be-
sides, with a singular tenacity of purpose and
mentally are capable of receiving a high education, which we may hope will be accepted with
moderation.

What will be their future when their
swamps are drained and their old lake-dweller
life merged into the humdrum of farmers? If by
good fortune they are kept from the deadly effects of alcohol, that chief moloch of the Mexican Indian, no doubt they will live happily on
the dry lake bottom as before in the days of
Montezuma.

THE FOREMOST INTELLECTUAL ACHIEVEMENT OF ANCIENT AMERICA

The Hieroglyphic Inscriptions on the Monuments in the Ruined Cities of Mexico, Guatemala, and Honduras Are Yielding the Secrets of the Maya Civilization

By Sylvanus Griswold Morley

Carnegie Institution of Washington, Author of "The Excavations at Quirigua, Guatemala," in the National Geographic Magazine

DURING the first millennium before Christ, while yet our own forebears of northern Europe were plunged in the depths of barbarism, there developed somewhere in Middle America, probably on the Gulf Coast of southern Mexico, a great aboriginal civilization called the Maya, which was destined to become the most brilliant expression of the ancient American mind.

Somewhat later, probably about the begin-ning of the Christian era, the Maya seem to have found their way into what is now the northern part of Guatemala, the Department of Peten, and the States of Chiapas and Tabasco, Mexico, and here for the next 600 years they flourished most amazingly.

During these centuries this highly gifted people, not inaptly called "the Greeks of the New World," were slowly fighting upward from savagery through barbarism to the threshold of civilization.

THE BALL COURT AT CHICHEN ITZA, YUCATAN

In this immense court, large as a foot-ball field, a game of ball was played called "tlachtli," not unlike our modern game of basket-ball. The player who succeeded in driving the ball through the ring attached to the center of each wall (that on the right is still in its original position) had forfeited to him by ancient custom of the game all the clothing and jewelry of the spectators.

Courtesy of The Carnegie Institution of Washington

A CHICLE (CHEWING-GUM) CAMP
IN A CLEARING IN THE FORESTS OF PETEN, GUATEMALA

These camps are located near aguadas, or water-holes, and are sometimes of a fairly permanent nature. The houses have palm-leaf thatched roofs and sides of boughs, and are thoroughly water-proof. A pile of chicle bales is seen in the foreground, each weighing from 100 to 150 pounds and being about the size of a large block of ice. The Carnegie Expedition's mule-train has just arrived at this camp; two mules are being unloaded at the left of the picture, and the table and cots are already set up for the night. Retiring in these forests is no light task, involving, as it does, the arrangement of an elaborate mosquito-netting and a search for stray insects with an electric torch before the process is complete.

AT THE RUINS OF IXLU, IN NORTHERN PETEN, GUATEMALA

The ruins of Ixlu were discovered on April 10, 1921. This photograph shows His Excellency Dr. José Prado Romaña, Governor of Peten; Mr. M. D. Bromberg, vice-president of the American Chicle Company, and several members of the Carnegie Central American Expedition staff on a visit of inspection to the newly discovered site, standing near one of the stone altars (see illustration on following page).

Their priests and astronomers were gathering from the stars the secrets of time and its accurate measure, the revolutions of the sun, moon, and planets; their mathematicians and chronologists were devising a calendar and chronology which was without peer on this continent and excelled by none in the Old World at that time; their builders were developing an architecture at once unique, dignified, and beautiful; their sculptors were carving the most elaborate compositions and designs in stone; their leaders had mastered the problems of social and governmental organization and were administering the state adequately and well. In short, a great national life was quickening to its fullest expression.

The zenith of their civilization, however—indeed, the intellectual climax of all civilizations—was the development of a hieroglyphic writing which, moreover, was the only system of writing in the New World worthy of comparison with the earlier graphic systems of the Old World, such as those of Egypt, of Babylonia, and of China, for example.

MAYA WRITINGS
TRANSFERRED TO STONE
BEFORE THE BIRTH OF CHRIST

This hieroglyphic writing was doubtless first developed upon wood, fiber-paper or skins, but shortly before the beginning of the Christian era it was transferred to stone, inscribed upon monuments and altars, which were erected in the courts and plazas in front of the principal temples of the different Maya cities.

And here, buried in the vast tropical forests of northern Central America, and especially in the State of Guatemala, these splendid memorials of a forgotten people are slowly coming to light.

Courtesy of The Carnegie Institution of Washington

THE ALTAR OF STELA 2, AT THE RUINS OF IXLU, PETEN, GUATEMALA

This beautiful example of Maya stone-carving, when first seen by Dr. Morley, on April 10, 1921, was tightly clasped in the roots of a large breadnut tree which was growing on top of it. When this tree was felled the next day and the altar beneath turned face upward for the first time in more than a thousand years, it was found to have six columns of hieroglyphs sculptured on its top in an almost perfect state of preservation, or 32 in all. It has been possible to decipher only the first five of these, namely, the first and second signs in the first column and the first, second, and third in the second column. These five, however, record the date of this altar as having been 10.2.10.0.0 2 Ahau 13 Chen of the Maya era (620 A. D.).

Courtesy of the School of American Research

THE CENOTE, OR GREAT POOL OF SACRIFICE, AT CHICHEN ITZA, YUCATAN

The ceremonies begun on the lofty summit of the Castillo had their ending at the brink of this great natural pool or well. The spot is solemn and awe-inspiring. A great hole in the earth, 225 feet in diameter, with perpendicular or undercut sides, dropping 70 feet to the level of the black, mysterious water below, is fringed on all sides by the dense tropical forests. Here the Maya, in times of drought, formerly brought their most beautiful maidens, and from a little platform near the small shrine at the left of the picture hurled them into the depths below. If any survived the tremendous shock of this great drop and struggled to the surface of the water, ropes were let down to them and they were hauled out, more dead than alive, we may well believe. Once again on *terra firma*, they were questioned by the priests as to what they had seen below? What the gods had in store for mankind? Would the following year bring forth rain and plenty or drought and famine? For these girls were believed to have found out the answers to these questions from the rain deities at the bottom of this pool.

Year after year archaeological expeditions sent out by American scientific institutions are penetrating deeper and deeper into these virgin fastnesses and are discovering new ruined cities, from the monuments and hieroglyphic inscriptions of which we are gradually reconstructing the outlines of ancient Maya history.

The only other business which brings man into these tropical forests of northern Guatemala is one of our most important American industries, what might be termed, perhaps, our national sport—chewing gum.

The principal ingredient of chewing gum is "chicle," which is obtained from a tree called the "chico-sapote," growing in these forests. Indeed, the archaeologist is deeply indebted to the chicle business for bringing him first news of new cities found in the bush from time to time by the chicle-hunters.

The writer has a standing reward offered to all *chicleros* for "information leading to the capture, dead or alive," of any new group of ruins where there are hieroglyphic monuments, and already this expedient has resulted in the discovery of several important cities.

It is the chicle-operators who keep the trails open; who locate the water-holes for camping-places; who maintain mule-trains, the only means of transportation possible in the region; whose activities bring labor into the bush. In short, in this field, at least, the archaeologist could scarcely pursue his profession were it not for our popular pastime of chewing gum. But to return to our subject.

MAYA WRITING REPRESENTS
TURNING POINT IN HUMAN HISTORY

The peculiar importance of the Maya hieroglyphic writing lies in the fact that it represents a stage in the science of expressing thoughts by graphic symbols not exemplified by the writing of any other people, ancient or modern. It stands at that momentous point in the development of the human race where graphic symbols representing sounds were just beginning to replace symbols representing ideas.

Man's first efforts at writing were doubtless as highly realistic as he could make them with his clumsy hands and still clumsier tools and drawing materials. If he wanted to express the idea "horse," he was obliged to draw the picture of a horse, since he had no symbols or characters by means of which the sound of its name could be indicated. In short, he was

THE TABLET FROM THE TEMPLE OF THE CROSS AT PALENQUE, MEXICO

This magnificent specimen of ancient Maya art is engraved upon three slabs of cream-colored limestone, which originally rested against the back wall of the sanctuary in the Temple of the Cross at Palenque, Chiapas, Mexico. In 1840 the American diplomat and traveler, John Lloyd Stephens, had the left-hand panel removed to the United States, where for more than half a century it remained in the Smithsonian Institution. Many years later the right-hand panel was removed to the National Museum in Mexico City, and still later the central panel, upon which the representation of a cross flanked by two officiating priests is carved, was also taken to the same place.

After the visit of former Secretary of State Root to Mexico, the panel in the Smithsonian Institution was returned to the Government of Mexico, a graceful act of international courtesy; so that now, after the lapse of nearly three-quarters of a century, the three panels of this beautiful aboriginal sculpture are again reunited in the National Museum in Mexico City.

obliged to convey the idea of a horse to the brain by means of the eye and not the ear—realistically—that is, by its picture—instead of phonetically, by its sound.

This earliest method of expressing thoughts graphically has been called ideographic writing because its symbols express ideas instead of sounds, as do the characters of our own alphabet.

It is obvious that this kind of writing has a very limited range, being able to express little more than concrete objects, and scarcely at all to convey action, save only by the clumsy makeshift of pictures representing specific acts; and man in the course of his development eventually devised a better method of expressing his thoughts than by merely drawing pictures of them.

BIRTH OF THE ALPHABET'S FIRST ANCESTOR

At this point we reach, for the first time, the introduction of the phonetic element into writing—that is to say, where a sign or character came to represent a sound, a syllable, or a letter and ceased to be a picture of an idea. And it is precisely at this important turning point in the history of writing that the Maya graphic system stands, representing, as stated previously, a stage in the development of writing found nowhere else in the world.

This change in the character of writing symbols, from signs representing ideas to signs representing sounds, was fundamental, and its far-reaching effects cannot be overstated. It soon made possible an enormous expansion in the subjects which could be expressed by writing, and it ultimately enabled mankind to write about everything he could talk or even think

about; in short, it reduced his universe to black and white—the written word.

Any graphic system, therefore, which stands at this crucial point in the evolution of writing is worthy of closer study and cannot be devoid of general interest, and in the following pages the writer has endeavored to present to the readers of the NATIONAL GEOGRAPHIC MAGAZINE a brief description of its principal characteristics.

AZTEC WRITING SIMPLER THAN THAT OF THE MAYA

However, before describing the Maya hieroglyphic writing, it will, perhaps, be easier to begin by describing the writing of the Aztec, the dominant Indian tribe of the Valley of Mexico, who had attained a high degree of civilization long before their conquest and practical annihilation by the Spaniards under Cortez, in 1521.

The Maya hieroglyphic writing was much older than that of the Aztec, and from the former the Aztec doubtless originally borrowed the idea of writing.

The Aztec writing is simpler than the Maya, and is better known, probably as high as 90 per cent of its signs and symbols having been deciphered. Their hieroglyphs may be divided into three groups, as follows:

1. Signs representing the calendar, such as the hieroglyphs for the days, months, and the year;

2. Signs representing the names of persons and places, such as the hieroglyphs for Montezuma and Tenochtitlan (the Aztec name for Mexico City);

3. Signs representing events or natural objects, such as the hieroglyphs for war, conquest, death, accession of rulers, festivals, eclipses,

EXAMPLE OF REBUS-WRITING: THE AZTEC HIEROGLYPHS
FOR PERSONAL AND PLACE NAMES WERE CONSTRUCTED ON THIS BASIS

The phonetic principle upon which rebus-writing is based is that of homophones—*i. e.*, words which sound alike or similar, but which have different meanings. The above rebus should be read: "I believe Aunt Rose can well bear all for you."

comets, earthquakes, volcanic eruptions, gold, jade, feathers, etc.

By means of these three groups of signs, painted in books made of fiber-paper or deerskin, the Aztec recorded the principal events of their history, not, to be sure, as long narratives glowing with eulogistic descriptions of the valorous deeds of kings and emperors, but as brief synopses of the principal events, none the less historically accurate, however, because of their brevity.

The Aztec calendar consisted of a year of 18 months of 20 days each, and a closing period of five days, into which it was believed all the bad luck of the year was crowded. No one started upon a journey during these five days, for fear some misfortune would befall him; no woodcutter ventured into the forest to hew wood during this period, lest wild beasts should devour him; the houses were left unswept; the housewives made no pottery vessels; children so unfortunate as to be born on one of these five days were by that very fact predestined to mis-

fortune for the rest of their lives; it was, in fact, the "Friday the 13th" of their year.

The next, and among the Aztec the only time period higher than the year, was the *xihuitlmolpia*, or cycle of 52 years. And if they believed thc closing five days of the year were fraught with ill luck, they regarded the closing night of their 52-year period with far greater terror, since it was held that at the close of one of these periods would some day come the destruction of the world.

AZTEC HIEROGLYPHS RESEMBLED REBUS-WRITING

On the last night of the xihuitlmolpia fires were extinguished on the hearths and the inhabitants of Tenochtitlan moved out of the city and took up positions on the surrounding hills, waiting feverishly either for the destruction of the world or, in the event of sunrise, the dawn of another xihuitlmolpia. Once the sun had arisen, however, great were the rejoicings. Fires were rekindled and the crisis was over for another 52 years.

The hieroglyphs for the names of persons and places, the second group mentioned previously, were built up on the basis of our own old-fashioned rebus-writing, an example of which is given on the next page. This depends upon the fact that many words of different meaning have the same or similar sounds, such as: to, too, two, bear, bare, reed, read, etc. In the rebus given above the pictures actually represent: an eye, a bee, a leaf, an ant, a rose, a can, a well, a bear, an awl, the number 4, and a ewe; but they may be transcribed as: "I believe Aunt Rose can well bear all for you." It was in this manner that the hieroglyphs for Aztec personal and place names were constructed.

HOW THE AZTEC RECORDED HISTORICAL EVENTS: THE ACCESSION OF MONTEZUMA

Finally, the third group of signs represented events and natural objects, such as death, war, conquest, accession of rulers, natural phenomena, gold, jade, etc. Thus a mummy-like human figure wrapped in cloths and tied with ropes represented death. A shield with javelins crossed behind it stood for war; a burning temple for conquest, etc.

The signs of this last group were the most limited in number, but they were at the same time of the most importance, since they alone gave point and life, as it were, to the characters of the other two groups.

Several examples of the Aztec hieroglyphic writing are given on pages 66, 67, and 68. The picture at the left on page 66 represents the death of the Aztec ruler Ahuitzotl in 1502 A. D. and the accession of his nephew, Montezuma II to the rulership of the tribe. At the top we see a circle, within which are a rabbit's head and 10 dots. This stands for the year 10 Tochtli or 10 Rabbit, corresponding to the year 1502 of the Christian era.

The Aztec had four different kinds of years: Reed, Flint, House, and Rabbit, named after the days (Reed, Flint, House, and Rabbit) with which they successively began. The numbers attached to these names, 1 to 13 inclusive, do not follow the sequence of our own numbers, so that the year 1 Flint follows the year 13 Reed.

Attached to the year 10 Rabbit, on the left, by a cord, there is the figure of a mummy bound with ropes and surmounted by a crown. This indicates the death of some ruler.

Another cord runs from the crown of this mummy to a small animal, from whose feet hang water symbols. This is the hieroglyph for Ahuitzotl, the Aztec word for water-animal. This much of our picture, then, records the death of the ruler Ahuitzotl in the year 10 Rabbit—*i. e.,* 1502 A. D.

To the right of this mummy there is a living figure, also attached to the circle above by a cord and also wearing the same crown. This right-hand figure is seated upon a dais, another emblem of Aztec royalty, and from its mouth there issues a scroll, the Aztec sign for supreme authority. The Aztec word for ruler was "tlahtouani," which means "he who speaks," shown graphically by a speech-scroll issuing from the mouth.

Finally, attached to the crown of the second figure is another crown, which is the hieroglyph for the name Montezuma, and the right-hand part of the picture is to be read: Montezuma became ruler in 1502.

THE RECORD OF A CONQUEST

Elliptical and abbreviated as this record is, it sets forth clearly that the ruler Ahuitzotl died in 1502 and was succeeded by Montezuma.

HISTORICAL EVENTS REPRESENTED IN THE AZTEC HIEROGLYPHIC MANUSCRIPTS

The drawing on the left shows the death of the Aztec ruler, Ahuitzotl, in the year 10 Rabbit (1502 A. D.) and the accession of his nephew, Montezuma II. The mummy of a human figure bound with ropes, with a crown on its head, indicates the death of a ruler, a mummy being the Aztec hieroglyph for death. The little water-animal attached to the crown by a cord shows that the dead ruler's name was Ahuitzotl, that being the Aztec word for "water-animal." The right half of this drawing shows a man seated upon a dais, with a crown upon his head and a speech-scroll issuing from. his mouth. The Aztec word for ruler was "tlahtouani," "he who speaks," shown graphically by the speech-scroll. Finally both figures are attached by cords to the circle above, which represents the year 10 Rabbit (1502 A. D.), indicating the date of this event.

The drawings at the center and right represent the conquest of Tehuantepec in the same year by Ahuitzotl shortly before his death. The year 10 Rabbit appears at the left, next the ruler Ahuitzotl, with the three emblems of Aztec royalty: the crown, the speech-scroll, and the dais with his name-hieroglyph, "Water-animal," above him. To the right and above is a shield with javelins crossed behind it, the hieroglyph for war; below the shield is a temple in flames, the hieroglyph for conquest. To the left of the temple is the hieroglyph for Tehuantepec, the head of a cat (tecuani) and a hill (tepec). The whole record might be paraphrased thus: In the year 10 Rabbit the ruler Ahuitzotl fought and conquered the town of Tehuantepec.

The second and third figures on this page represent the conquest of the town of Tehuantepec by the Aztec ruler Ahuitzotl shortly before his death, in 1502. In the square at the left hand is the year 10 Rabbit, which corresponded, as explained previously, to the year 1502. Next Ahuitzotl is portrayed with the three emblems of Aztec royalty—the crown, the dais, and the speech-scroll. His name glyph, "The Water-animal," appears above, attached to his head by a cord.

The shield with the javelins behind it is the Aztec hieroglyph for war (at the right, above), and the temple in flames (note the smoke curls) denotes conquest.

The name of the town conquered appears to the left of the burning temple; it is the head of a man-eating cat, possibly the jaguar, surmounting a hill: *tecuani*, a "man-eating cat," and *tepec*, "hill or town." This picture, therefore, is to be interpreted as recording the conquest of the town of Tehuantepec, in southern Mexico, on the isthmus of the same name, by the ruler Ahuitzotl in 1502.

THE RECORD OF A TEMPLE'S DEDICATION

The picture on page 67 portrays the dedication of the great temple of Huitzilipochtli, the Aztec God of War, at Tenochtitlan, in 1484, at

DEDICATION OF THE GREAT TEMPLE OF HUITZILIPOCHTLI, THE AZTEC GOD OF WAR, AT TENOCHTITLAN, IN THE YEAR 5 FLINT (1484 A. D.)

The year 5 Flint is represented in the square above by the flint with the five dots on its right. Below is the great temple of the War God, its stairway red with the blood of the sacrificial victims. On top of the pyramid is the hieroglyph for Tenochtitlan, the ancient name of Mexico City, expressed by a stone with a cactus growing out of it. On the right is a priest in the act of despatching one of the human victims. This event took place in the second year of the reign of Tizoc, the seventh Aztec ruler, and it is said to have been the first occasion when human sacrifice was practiced by the Aztec, previously to this the sacrifices having been of animals and birds.

which human sacrifice is said to have been practiced for the first time. In the square above is a piece of flint and five dots, representing the year 5 Tecpatl, or 5 Flint, corresponding to 1484 A. D. To this is attached, on the right, the figure of a priest who has just sacrificed a human victim, the latter pictured as dying on the ground, weltering in his own blood.

To the left is the great temple of the War God, the stairway being shown as plentifully besprinkled with the gore of the hecatomb of vic-

tims. On top of the pyramid is a stone from which grows a cactus, this combination being the hieroglyph for Tenochtitlan.

HOW THE AZTEC RECORDED AN ECLIPSE

Figure *a* on page 68 shows an eclipse of the sun which was visible in the Valley of Mexico in 1510. Again the year is shown by the rabbit's head and the five dots in the square above— *i. e.*, 5 Tochtli, or 5 Rabbit (1510), from which hangs the sun's disk with a sector bitten out of it, the Aztec hieroglyph denoting an eclipse.

Figure *b* on page 68 represents a comet which swept over Mexico in 1489. Above, the year 10 Calli, or 10 House, is recorded, which corresponded with the year 1489 of the Christian era. Attached to the year is the hieroglyph for a comet, happily represented by the Aztec as a large serpent stretching across the heavens.

Montezuma regarded this comet as an evil omen, presaging the downfall of himself and his race; so that three decades later, when Cortez landed in Mexico, the superstitious Indian ruler thought that the fair-skinned Spaniards were sons of the white-skinned, golden-haired Aztec god, Quetzalcoatl, and pursued such a vacillatory policy toward the invaders that his empire was speedily destroyed and his people enslaved forever.

AN EARTHQUAKE ACCOMPANIED BY A VOLCANIC ERUPTION

The third figure, *c*, on page 68, shows an earthquake accompanied by a volcanic eruption, which occurred in the Valley of Mexico in 1533. Above we see the year 2 Calli, or 2 House, corresponding to 1533 A. D. Below is a star, above which smoke scrolls are rising. The Aztec word for a volcanic eruption is smoke as-

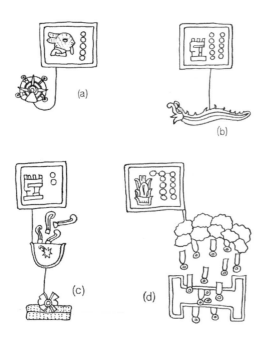

NATURAL PHENOMENA RECORDED IN THE AZTEC HIEROGLYPHIC MANUSCRIPTS

(*a*) An eclipse of the sun which took place in the year 5 Rabbit (1510 A. D.). The year is represented by the rabbit's head and the five dots in the square above, and the eclipse of the sun by the picture of the sun's disk with a sector bitten out of it.

(*b*) A comet which swept over the Valley of Mexico in the year 10 House (1489 A. D.). The year is represented in the square above and the comet by the serpent below.

(*c*) A volcanic eruption and earthquake in the year 2 House (1533 A. D.). The year appears in the square above. Below is a star with smoke curls rising above it, the sign for a volcanic eruption, the Aztec word for which is "smoke ascending to the stars." Below is the sign for an earthquake, a sort of winged eye, meaning "movement" (Aztec ollin), applied to the earth, the speckled rectangle.

(*d*) A heavy fall of snow which occurred in the province of Tlachquiahco in the year 11 Reed (1503 A. D.). The year appears above. The bank of clouds indicates the snow, and the H-shaped object below, covered with water symbols, is the hieroglyph for the province of Tlachquiahco.

cending to the stars, and this is the sign for it. At the bottom is a sign which means "movement" (ollin), applied to a speckled band which represents the earth, and a "movement of the earth" is very emphatically an earthquake.

Figure *d* on this page represents a heavy fall of snow which occurred in the town of Tlachquiahco in 1503.

Above is the year 11 Acatl, or 11 Reed (1503), to which is attached a great bank of clouds, the snow. Below is an H-shaped object, the Aztec ball-court, *tlachtli*, covered with water symbols, *quiahuitl*, the rain; the combination of the two giving *tlach* (tli) *quiah* (uitl), the parts in parentheses being omitted in combination and the *co* being added as indicating a place: Tlachquiahco.

It was by means of such simple symbols as these, and all told there were not so many of them, that the Aztec were able to set forth the principal events of their history, to record and date the accessions and deaths of their rulers, their wars and conquests, and the tributes exacted from the conquered cities and towns of Anahuac (the ancient name for central Mexico).

They noted important religious ceremonials and extraordinary natural phenomena—earthquakes, volcanic eruptions, comets, and the like—and, finally, famines, pestilences, and migrations.

MAYA WRITING FAR MORE COMPLEX

In short, the Aztec hieroglyphic writing, of which we now read about 90 per cent of the characters, gives only a skeleton of history, the barest outline of principal events; but as for detailed descriptions, extended narratives, there are none—in fact, such were quite beyond the compass of its limited and simple symbols to express.

LUNCH AT THE RUINS OF NARANJO, PETEN, GUATEMALA

After a hot morning's work stumbling through the dense bush in search of new monuments, lunch taken on top of one of them is very grateful.

Courtesy of The Carnegie Institution of Washington

DRAWING A HIEROGLYPHIC INSCRIPTION
ON A NEWLY TURNED MONUMENT IN PETEN

The figure on the monument is not posing for his picture, but was caught unaware by the expedition photographer while engaged in the intricacies of deciphering a newly found hieroglyphic inscription.

The Maya hieroglyphic writing presents greater problems in decipherment. To begin with, its characters are much more numerous, probably twice as many as in the Aztec writing, and at the same time they are much more complex.

Again, the Spanish priests and chroniclers of the 16th century have described at consider-able length the Aztec graphic system, whereas only one authority, Bishop Diego de Landa, has written anything detailed about the Maya writing. And, finally, although nearly two score Aztec hieroglyphic manuscripts or books have come down to us, only three Maya ones have been found: The Dresden Codex, at the Royal Library at Dresden; the Tro-Cortesianus Co-

Courtesy of The Carnegie Institution of Washington

CHICLE HUNTERS RETURNING HOME
AT THE END OF THE CHICLE SEASON EARLY IN THE SPRING

The milk of the chico-sapote tree, from which chewing-gum is made, runs only during the rainy season, from June to January, inclusive, during which time the chicle-bleeders are in the bush. At the end of the season they return to their homes for three or four months, to spend in a fortnight all they have so laboriously earned during the past seven or eight months, and then to live on credit until the beginning of the next season. This picture shows a group of 150 chicle-bleeders being picked up at a camp on the San Pedro Martir River, in Peten, to be carried down stream to their various villages. They travel with all conceivable impedimenta, from an umbrella to a pet monkey, and are of both sexes and all ages.

REPRESENTATION OF A BLOOD-LETTING CEREMONY

This sculptured panel, now in the British Museum, was originally carved on the under side of a door lintel in one of the temples of the great Maya city of Yaxchilan, in southern Mexico. A priest with a ceremonial staff is shown at the left, supervising a blood-letting ceremony, possibly by a neophyte, who is kneeling at the right. Note the gorgeous details of the priest's costume. The neophyte, scarcely less handsomely garbed, is engaged in drawing blood from himself by passing through a slit in his tongue a long piece of rope with sharp thorns fastened to it. A basin on the ground catches the drops of blood as they fall.

Courtesy of The Carnegie Institution of Washington

ALTAR 2, AT THE RUINS OF CANCUEN, GUATEMALA

This altar was discovered in 1915, at the ruins of Cancuen, on the east bank of the Pasión River, in southern central Peten. It is 2 feet in diameter and 7 inches in thickness and the sculpture on the top represents two priests officiating at an altar (the disk between them). The first two hieroglyphs at the top give its date as 9.18.5.0.0 4 Ahau 13 Ceh of the Maya era (536 A. D.).

dex, at the Royal Academy of History, Madrid, and the Peresianus Codex, at the Biblioteque National, Paris.

These several factors have made the problems involved in its complete decipherment more difficult than that of the Aztec, and have left us more in the dark as to the subjects covered in the Maya inscriptions.

The Maya hieroglyphic writing is composed of about 400 different characters or elements, of which probably as high as 90 to 95 per cent are ideographic rather than phonetic, as has been explained.

These four hundred odd basic elements, however, are combined in about half as many common compound characters, about half of which in turn have been deciphered; so that it may be fairly claimed that the Maya inscriptions no longer are a sealed book to us. Although much remains to be done in this important line of investigation, already enough characters have had their meanings determined so that we begin to catch the general drift of these records, even if the details still escape us.

MARVELOUS ACCURACY
SHOWN IN MAYA CALENDAR

So far as the Maya inscriptions have been deciphered, they deal exclusively with the counting of time in one phase or another. They record with extraordinary accuracy the dates of the monuments upon which they are engraved, so that no confusion exists between any two days within a period of more than 370,000 years.

They set forth elaborate lunar or moon calendars, in which the lunar month, involving a very difficult fractional number, is delicately and exactly coördinated with the solar calendar over long periods of time. They predict eclipses and correctly record the movements and phases of the planets, especially Venus; and, in addition to the foregoing, there is a wealth of other chronological data of as yet unknown significance.

Whether this last refers to historical events or astronomical phenomena has not yet been determined, though doubtless the still undeciphered hieroglyphs will clear up this point when their meanings shall have been worked out.

It is evident from the foregoing that the element of time was of primary importance to the ancient Maya, and that its record, as variously manifested by the sun, moon, and planets, fills a large part of their inscriptions.

MAYA ARITHMETIC

Let us next examine, then, some of the features of Maya arithmetic and see how these chronological and astronomical facts were expressed.

First, the Maya, like ourselves, had two different ways of writing their numbers, one by bars and dots, and the other by different types of the human head. The former may be likened to our Roman numerals, and the latter to our Arabic numerals.

The Maya "Roman notation" made use of but two elements, the dot standing for the number 1 and the bar standing for the number 5. In this respect, at least, their bar and dot numerals were even simpler than our Roman numbers, since we have to use seven letters—I, V, X, L, C, D, and M—in the Roman notation. By various combinations of these two elements, in which the dot had the value of 1 and the bar of 5, the Maya wrote the numbers from 1 to 19, inclusive (see the examples of bar and dot numerals on page 74).

The Maya "Arabic notation" made use of 13 different types of human heads to express the numbers 1 to 13, inclusive; and then, by apply-

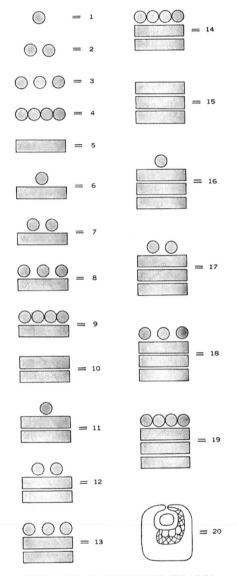

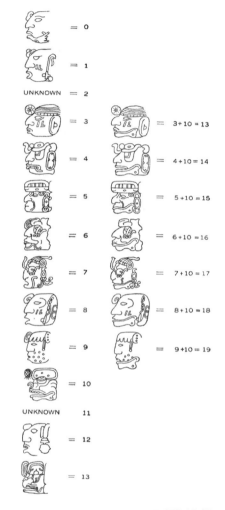

THE MAYA "ROMAN NUMERALS"

In the Maya bar and dot numerals, the dot stands for 1 and the bar for 5. These elements, when added together in the proper combinations, give the numbers from 6 to 19, inclusive. The number 20 is shown at the bottom of the second column. It is also the hieroglyph for the moon.

THE MAYA "ARABIC NUMERALS"

In the Maya head numerals there are 14 different types of human heads, representing the numbers from 0 to 13, inclusive, although the heads for two of these numbers, 2 and 11, have not yet been deciphered. The numerals from 13 to 19, inclusive, were formed by adding the essential characteristic of the head for 10—i. e., the fleshless lower jaw—to the heads for 3 to 9, inclusive. Thus, for example, adding the fleshless lower jaw of the head for 10 to the head for 6, characterized by the "crossed bands" in the eye, gives the head for 16, viz., 10 + 6 = 16.

ing the essential characteristic of the head for 10, a fleshless lower jaw to the heads for 4, 5, 6, 7, 8, and 9, they formed the numbers 14, 15, 16, 17, 18, and 19, respectively (see the examples of head numerals on the opposite page).

One peculiar feature of this notation was the use of two kinds of heads for the number 13—the simple form shown at the bottom of the first column on the right side of page 74, and the compound form, 3 + 10, shown at the top of the second column. The use of the latter, however, was very rare, there not being more than two or three examples of it known.

The higher numbers were expressed by positions from bottom to top in a column. Just as in our decimal system the positions increase by a ratio of 10 from left or right of the decimal point, viz., units, tens, hundreds, thousands, etc., so the Maya positions increased by a ratio of 20 from bottom to top in a column, in all places except the third, which, instead of being 400, $i.\ e.$, $1 \times 20 \times 20$, was 360, $i.\ e.$, $1 \times 20 \times 18$. This single break in an otherwise perfect vigesimal system of numeration was doubtless due to the desire to bring its third term as near to the length of the solar year as possible, 360 being much nearer to 365¼ than 400. Examples of higher numbers are given on page 76.

LITTLE OR NO HISTORICAL MATTER IN MAYA WRITINGS

It was stated that in so far as they have been deciphered, and it is now possible to read nearly one-half of the Maya hieroglyphs, the Maya inscriptions have been found to deal exclusively with the counting of time in one way or another.

No grandiloquent record of earthly glory these. No bombastic chronicles of kingly pomp and pageantry, like most of the Assyrian, Baby-

lonian, and Egyptian inscriptions. On the contrary, the Maya priests would seem to have been concerned with more substantial matters, such as the observation and record of astronomical phenomena. Of first importance to them would appear to have been the dates of the many monuments they erected.

These dates are usually recorded at the beginnings of the inscriptions, and are frequently of such accuracy as to fix their positions within a period of some 370,000 years, surely not an inconsiderable achievement for any time-count, even one of modern origin.

THE MAYA ERECTED THEIR MONUMENTS AT INTERVALS OF EVERY 1,800 DAYS

The Maya monuments, it has been ascertained from their dates, were erected at intervals of every 1,800 days—nearly five years. This custom seems to have been so general that on several occasions, when monuments commemorating specific 5-year periods at certain cities were missing, it has been possible, first to predict their existence and later to have found them. Indeed, these intricately carved monoliths are probably to be regarded as little more than 5-year almanacs in stone, which set forth not only the dates of their erection or dedication, but also important lunar and planetary phenomena as well.

An example of this kind occurred at the ruins of Piedras Negras last May. After the Carnegie Expedition had been at this site a week, it was found that there was a corresponding monument for every 5-year period from 378 to 536 A. D., save only for the 5-year period ending in 487 A. D.

The writer, on the basis of this condition, predicted that a monument would surely be

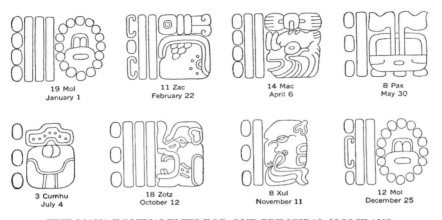

| 19 Mol
January 1 | 11 Zac
February 22 | 14 Mac
April 6 | 8 Pax
May 30 |
| 3 Cumhu
July 4 | 18 Zotz
October 12 | 8 Xul
November 11 | 12 Mol
December 25 |

THE MAYA EQUIVALENTS FOR OUR PRINCIPAL HOLIDAYS

Every day of the Maya year had its corresponding hieroglyph. In 1566, when Bishop Landa wrote his famous "History of the Things of Yucatan," the Maya year began on July 16 (Old Style) or July 26 (New Style). On the basis of this correlation the Mayan equivalents for some of our principal holidays are given above, the numbers in bars and dots at the left indicating the positions in the months, and the signs to the right the names of the corresponding Maya months.

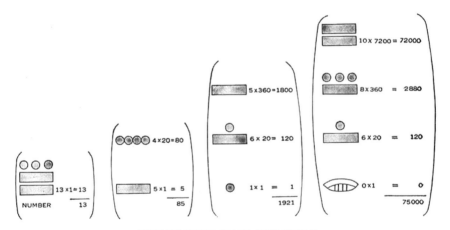

THE HIGHER MAYA NUMBERS

Our own arithmetical system is decimal, the values of the terms increasing from left or right of the decimal point in a ratio of 10. The Maya arithmetical system was vigesimal—that is, the values of the terms increased from bottom to top in a ratio of 20, except in the case of the third term, which was 360 (*i. e.*, 1 × 20 × 18) instead of 400 (*i. e.*, 1 × 20 × 20). This break in an otherwise perfect vigesimal system was probably due to the desire to bring its third term as near to the length (of the solar year as possible.

The first number above is 13, *i. e.*, 13 units of the first order, or 13 × 1. The second number is 85, which the Maya wrote as 5 units of the first order, or 5, and 4 units of the second order, or 4 × 1 × 20 = 80; and 5 + 80 = 85. The third number is 1,921, *i. e.*, 1 unit of the first order, 6 units of the second order (6 × 1 × 20 = 120), and 5 units of the third order (5 × 1 × 20 × 18 = 1,800); all of which, added together, give 1 + 120 + 1,800 = 1,921. The fourth number is 75,000, *i. e.*, 0 units of the first order, 6 units of the second order (6 × 1 × 20 = 120), 8 units of the third order (8 × 1 × 20 × 18 = 2,880), and 10 units of the fourth order (10 × 1 × 20 × 18 × 20 = 72,000); all of which, added together, give 0 + 120 + 2,880 + 72,000 = 75,000. By this method the Maya could write numbers as high as 64,000,000.

THE PRINCIPAL GODS OF THE ANCIENT MAYA

There were not less than twelve major deities in the Maya Pantheon. The four most important are represented here with their name hieroglyphs below them. From left to right they are: Itzamna, the Mayan Jupiter and the Father of Mankind; Kukulcan, the Feathered Serpent, Culture Hero of the Itza nation;. Ahpuch, the Lord of Death (note the fleshless lower jaw used in the head numbers for 10, 14, 15, 16, 17, 18, and 19); and Yum Kax, Lord of the Harvest, his head-dress representing a conventionalized ear of corn.

found bearing this date; and on May 22 Mr. O. G. Ricketson, Jr., who was mapping the city, discovered the beautiful stela shown on page 79, which the inscription on its side shows was erected in 9. 15. 15. 0. 0 9 Ahau 18 Xul (487 A. D.), thus making the series of period-markers at this city complete for 158 years.

This new monument, which was named Stela 40, is 16 feet high, 4 feet wide, and 1½ feet in thickness. It represents Yum Kax, Lord of the Harvests, sowing corn. The God is seen dropping grains of corn from his extended right hand, the left holding the bag from which he has taken them. His head-dress, in keeping with his character of the Corn God, is a conventionalized ear of corn. Below there is a large human head and shoulders upon which the corn is falling. Could this have been a Maya conception of the Earth Mother receiving the seed she is to fructify?

"THE HOTUN," A GREAT NATIONAL HOLIDAY

This prediction of the existence of monuments in advance of their actual discovery has been repeated elsewhere, notably at Quirigua and Naranjo, where the sequence of the 5-year period-markers was at first incomplete, as in the case of Piedras Negras, subsequent discoveries, however, having filled in the gaps. Indeed, the writer regards the discovery of the principle which governed the erection of the Maya monuments, namely the 5-year interval, as one of the most important contributions to the subject during the past decade.

A name has been invented for this period, "hotun," the Maya word for "5 tuns" or 5 of

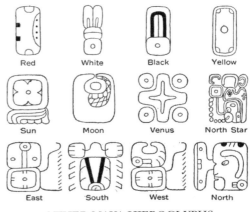

OTHER MAYA HIEROGLYPHS

Top row, certain colors; middle row, certain heavenly bodies; bottom row, the cardinal points.

FOUR MAYA MONUMENTS OF DIFFERENT AGES,
SHOWING THE DEVELOPMENT OF STONE-CARVING DURING THE OLD MAYA EMPIRE

The first monument (Stela 3, at Tical) dates from 229 A. D.; the second (Stela 25, at Naranjo) is 125 years later, dating from 354 A. D.; the third (Stela B, at Copan) is 118 years later than the second, dating from 472 A. D.; the fourth (Stela 10, at Seibal) is 118 years later than the third and dates from 590 A. D.

Courtesy of The Carnegie Institution of Washington

THE CORN GOD SOWING GRAINS OF THE MAYA STAFF OF LIFE

This is one of the finest examples of Maya stone-carving that has come down to us. It was discovered May 22, 1921, at the city of Piedras Negras, Guatemala (see text, page 77).

DESTRUCTION OF THE WORLD BY FLOOD AS REPRESENTED IN A MAYA HIEROGLYPHIC MANUSCRIPT

The above illustration shows the destruction of the world by water as depicted in the Dresden Codex (see page 70).

Across the sky stretches a great serpent belching forth torrents of water. From his body hang the sun and moon, both shown as in eclipse (note the black and white wings on each side of them), streams of water also pouring down from them.

Below the serpent is the old Tiger-clawed Goddess with a snake head-dress. On her skirt is broidered a pair of cross-bones—our own modern symbol for death. She holds a water-jar upside down, from which gushes another torrent of water.

Finally, below is the Black Captain, the Maya God of War, the Moan, a bird of ill omen, perched upon his head, down-pointing arrows and a javelin in his hands.

their 360-day periods, and its hieroglyph has been identified.

The prevalence of this practice of erecting period-markers throughout the Old Empire and its persistence down to the time of the Spanish Conquest, in 1541, calls up an interesting picture. We may imagine the closing day of these 5-year periods as great religious festivals. The inhabitants from the surrounding countryside gathered in the nearest city to attend the dedication of the monument, which had been prepared so laboriously and painstakingly under the supervision of the priests during the previous five years.

They could not read the hieroglyphic writing, it is true, but during the dedication ceremonies the priests doubtless informed them of the various astronomical phenomena of which they treated. With prayers to the gods for rain and fertility, with sacrifices and probably religious dances, the current period-marker was formally dedicated, perhaps we may even say "unveiled."

A parallel case would be as if on the 31st of December every fifth year, say in 1915, in 1920, in 1925, the inhabitants of our larger cities should congregate in the principal squares or plazas of their respective centers, and under their city authorities and clergy formally dedicate monuments commemorating the principal events of the past 5 years, this same ceremony being held all over the country on the same day. It was in fact a great national festival, possibly indeed the greatest national holiday of the ancient Maya.

When it is remembered that all the beautiful carvings found on these period-markers were made with tools of stone only, since the Maya of that time had no metals, the magni-

tude of their achievement grows and we are lost in wonder at the ingenuity and brilliance of this great native American people.

THE MAYA INSCRIPTIONS PRINCIPALLY ASTRONOMICAL AND CHRONOLOGICAL

It is becoming increasingly apparent, as we press our way into the meaning of the still undeciphered hieroglyphs, that they deal more and more with the subject-matter of astronomy and less and less with that of history. So much so, in fact, that if historical data be present at all on the Maya monuments, they must be confined to brief allusions to the more important events, as in the case of the Aztec manuscripts already described.

And it must be remembered in this connection that no Maya signs of abstract general meaning, like those in group 3 of the Aztec signs, have as yet been deciphered, and only a very few of group 2, namely, the signs for the names of the principal deities (see page 77).

If, therefore, as now seems probable, we must abandon the idea that the ancient Maya recorded history in their inscriptions, save only in very abbreviated and synoptical allusions to the more important events, we may, on the other hand, console ourselves with the reflection that possibly they were more worthily employed in recording matters of scientific moment, such as the movements of the heavenly bodies.

So accurate, indeed, would appear to have been their observations in this particular field that before long we shall probably know the ages of the different Maya cities more exactly than we will ever know the ages of Babylon,

Nineveh, Memphis, Thebes, Athens, or even of Imperial Rome herself.

MAYA CHRONOLOGY, THE TIME "YARDSTICK" FOR ALL ASSOCIATED CULTURES

Finally, this greatest aboriginal American writing provides us with a system of counting time, a chronological yardstick, as it were, by means of which it will eventually be possible to date all the contiguous ancient American civilizations as far south as the great cultures of Peru, the Inca, etc., and as far north as the Pueblo culture of our own Southwest.

Indeed, the writer regards it as not only possible, but even probable, that the comprehensive excavations now being undertaken by the National Geographic Society at Pueblo Bonito, Chaco Cañon, New Mexico, may at any time bring to light specimens, pieces of pottery brought in by trade in ancient times from central Mexico, which in turn will be datable in the Maya chronological system, and hence in our own Christian era.

THE LUSTER OF ANCIENT MEXICO

The following article is abstracted from the celebrated classic,
"History of the Conquest of Mexico," by William H. Prescott

O F ALL that extensive empire which once acknowledged the authority of Spain in the New World, no portion, for interest and importance, can be compared with Mexico, and this equally, whether we consider the variety of its soil and climate; the inexhaustible stores of its mineral wealth; its scenery, grand and picturesque beyond example; the character of its ancient inhabitants, not only far surpassing in intelligence that of the other North American races, but reminding us, by their monuments, of the primitive civilization of Egypt and Hindostan; or, lastly, the peculiar circumstances of its conquest, adventurous and romantic as any legend devised by Norman or Italian bard of chivalry.

The country of the ancient Mexicans, or Aztecs, as they were called, formed but a very small part of the extensive territories comprehended in the modern Republic of Mexico. Its boundaries cannot be defined with certainty. They were much enlarged in the latter days of the empire, when they may be considered as reaching from about the eighteenth degree north to the twenty-first, on the Atlantic, and from the fourteenth to the nineteenth, including a very narrow strip, on the Pacific. In its greatest breadth it could not exceed five degrees and a half, dwindling, as it approached its southeastern limits, to less than two.

It covered probably less than 16,000 square leagues. Yet such is the remarkable formation of this country that, though not more than twice as large as New England, it presented every variety of climate, and was capable of yielding nearly every fruit found between the Equator and the Arctic Circle.

All along the Atlantic the country is bordered by a broad tract, called the *tierra caliente*, or hot region, which has the usual high temperature of equinoctial lands. Parched and sandy plains are intermingled with others of exuberant fertility, almost impervious from thickets of aromatic shrubs and wild flowers, in the midst of which tower up trees of that magnificent growth which is found only within the tropics.

SCENERY GRAND AND TERRIBLE

After passing some twenty leagues across this burning region, the traveler finds himself rising into a purer atmosphere. His limbs recover their elasticity. He breathes more freely, for his senses are not now oppressed by the sultry heat and intoxicating perfumes of the valley. The aspect of nature, too, has changed, and his eye no longer revels among the gay variety of colors with which the landscape was painted there. The vanilla, the indigo, and the flowering cacao groves disappear as he advances. The sugarcane and the glossy-leaved banana still accompany him; and, when he has ascended about 4,000 feet, he sees in the unchanging verdure and the rich foliage of the liquid-amber tree that he has reached the height where clouds and mists settle in their passage from the Mexican Gulf.

He has entered the *tierra templada*, or temperate region, whose character resembles that of the temperate zone of the globe. The features of the scenery become grand and even terrible. His road sweeps along the base of mighty mountains, once gleaming with volcanic fires, and still resplendent in their mantles of snow, which serve as beacons to the mariner, for many a league at sea. All around he beholds traces of their ancient combustion, as his road passes along vast tracts of lava, bristling in the innumerable fantastic forms into which the fiery torrent has been thrown by the obstacles in its career. Perhaps at the same moment as he casts his eye down some steep slope or almost unfathomable ravine on the margin of the road he sees their depths glowing with the rich blooms and enameled vegetation of the tropics. Such are the singular contrasts presented, at the same time, to the senses in this picturesque region!

Still pressing upward, the traveler mounts into other climates, favorable to other kinds of cultivation. The yellow maize, or Indian corn, as we usually call it, has continued to follow him up from the lowest level; but he now first sees fields of wheat and the other European grains brought into the country by the Conquerors. Mingled with them he views the plantations of the aloe or maguey (*agave Americana*), applied to such various and important uses by the Aztecs. The oaks now acquire a sturdier growth, and the dark forests of pine announce that he has entered the *tierra fria*, or cold region, the third and last of the great natural terraces into which the country is divided.

THE BROAD MEXICAN TABLE-LAND

When he has climbed to the height of between 7,000 and 8,000 feet, the weary traveler sets his foot on the summit of the Cordillera of the Andes—the colossal range that, after traversing South America and the Isthmus of Darien, spreads out as it enters Mexico into that vast sheet of table-land, which maintains an elevation of more than 6,000 feet, for the distance of nearly 200 leagues, until it gradually declines in the higher latitudes of the north.

The air is exceedingly dry; the soil, though naturally good, is rarely clothed with the luxuriant vegetation of the lower regions. It frequently, indeed, has a parched and barren aspect, owing partly to the greater evaporation which takes place on these lofty plains, through the diminished pressure of the atmosphere; and partly, no doubt, to the want of trees to shelter the soil from the fierce influence of the summer sun.

In the time of the Aztecs the table-land was thickly covered with larch, oak, cypress, and other forest trees, the extraordinary dimensions of some of which, remaining to the present day, show that the curse of barrenness in later times is chargeable more on man than on nature. Indeed, the early Spaniards made as indiscriminate war on the forest as did our Puritan ancestors, though with much less reason. After once conquering the country they had no lurking ambush to fear from the submissive, semi-civilized Indian, and were not, like our forefathers, obliged to keep watch and ward for a century. This spoliation of the ground, however, is said to have been pleasing to their imagi-

COLIMA, ONE OF MEXICO'S ACTIVE VOLCANOES

On the sides of this great safety valve of the big earth furnace are numerous ice camps. Hail forms and falls so continuously here that the peons gather up the ice-stones, wrap them in straw, and carry them down to the towns on the plain for domestic purposes.

GATHERING PRICKLY PEAR FRUIT
NEAR THE PYRAMID OF THE SUN: SAN JUAN TEOTIHUACAN, MEXICO

The nopal cactus bears the tuna of the Mexicans and the prickly pear of Americans. The tree is composed of series of oval pads. As one of these pads hardens, it becomes a part of the tree instead of remaining its foliage and fruit. The great pad produces a fruit about the size of a duck egg, covered with fine prickles, as full of seeds as the ordinary fig. It is always cool when plucked. The natives subsist almost entirely on it when they can get it.

85

nations, as it reminded them of the plains of their own Castile, where the nakedness of the landscape forms the burden of every traveler's lament who visits that country.

THE WONDERFUL VALLEY OF MEXICO

Midway across the continent, somewhat nearer the Pacific than the Atlantic Ocean, at an elevation of nearly 7,500 feet, is the celebrated Valley of Mexico. It is of an oval form, about 67 leagues in circumference, and is encompassed by a towering rampart of porphyritic rock, which nature seems to have provided, though ineffectually, to protect it from invasion.

The soil, once carpeted with a beautiful verdure, and thickly sprinkled with stately trees, is often bare, and in many places, white with the incrustation of salts, caused by the draining of the waters. Five lakes are spread over the valley, occupying one-tenth of its surface. On the opposite borders of the largest of these basins, much shrunk in its dimensions since the days of the Aztecs, stood the cities of Mexico and Tezcuco, the capitals of the two most potent and flourishing States of Anahuac, whose history, with that of the mysterious races that preceded them in the country, exhibits some of the nearest approaches to civilization to be met with anciently on the North American continent.

Of these races the most conspicuous were the Toltecs. Advancing from a northerly direction, but from what region is uncertain, they entered the territory of Anahuac, probably before the close of the seventh century.

The Toltecs were well instructed in agriculture, and many of the most useful mechanic arts; were nice workers of metals; invented the complex arrangement of time adopted by the Aztecs; and, in short, were the true fountains of the civilization which distinguished this part of the continent in later times. They established their capital at Tula, north of the Mexican Valley, and the remains of extensive buildings were to be discerned there at the time of the Conquest. The noble ruins of religious and other edifices, still to be seen in various parts of New Spain, are referred to this people, whose name, *Toltec*, has passed into a synonym for *architect*. Their shadowy history reminds us of those primitive races who preceded the ancient Egyptians in the march of civilization, fragments of whose monuments, as they are seen at this day, incorporated with the buildings of the Egyptians themselves, give to these latter the appearance of almost modern constructions.

DID THE TOLTECS BUILD MITLA AND PALENQUE?

After a period of four centuries, the Toltecs, who had extended their sway over the remotest borders of Anahuac, having been greatly reduced, it is said, by famine, pestilence, and unsuccessful wars, disappeared from the land as silently and mysteriously as they had entered it. A few of them still lingered behind, but much the greater number, probably, spread over the region of Central America and the neighboring isles; and the traveler now speculates on the majestic ruins of Mitla and Palenque, as possibly the work of this extraordinary people.

The Mexicans, with whom our history is principally concerned, came, also, from the remote regions of the north—the populous hive of nations in the New World, as it has been in the Old. They arrived on the borders of Anahuac, toward the beginning of the thirteenth century, some time after the occupation of the land by the kindred races. For a long time they did not establish themselves in any permanent residence, but continued shifting their quarters

TARAHUMARE INDIANS IN CHIHUAHUA CITY, MEXICO

Not even Greece and Rome in the palmiest days of their athletic history produced a race of greater physical endurance than is to be found in the Tarahumare Indians of Mexico. Their favorite pastime is chasing a big ball, which they sometimes do from morning to night. Lumholtz, in his "Unknown Mexico," says they can run down and catch wild horses, and that the women are as good runners as the men.

to different parts of the Mexican Valley, enduring all the casualties and hardships of a migratory life. On one occasion they were enslaved by a more powerful tribe, but their ferocity soon made them formidable to their masters.

THE FOUNDING OF TENOCHTITLAN

After a series of wanderings and adventures, which need not shrink from comparison with the most extravagant legends of the he-

roic ages of antiquity, they at length halted on the southwestern borders of the principal lake in the year 1325. They there beheld, perched on the stem of a prickly pear, which shot out from the crevice of a rock that was washed by the waves, a royal eagle of extraordinary size and beauty, with a serpent in his talons, and his broad wings opened to the rising sun.

They hailed the auspicious omen, announced by the oracle as indicating the site of their future city, and laid its foundations by sinking piles into the shallows, for the low marshes were half buried under water. On these they erected their light fabrics of reeds and rushes, and sought a precarious subsistence from fishing and from the wild fowl which frequented the waters, as well as from the cultivation of such simple vegetables as they could raise on their floating gardens. The place was called Tenochtitlan, in token of its miraculous origin, though only known to Europeans by its other name of Mexico, derived from their wargod, Mexitli. The legend of its foundation is still further commemorated by the device of the eagle and the cactus, which form the arms of the modern Mexican Republic.

They gradually increased, however, in numbers, and strengthened themselves yet more by various improvements in their polity and military discipline, while they established a reputation for courage as well as cruelty in war, which made their name terrible throughout the Valley. In the early part of the fifteenth century, nearly a hundred years from the foundation of the city, an event took place which created an entire revolution in the circumstances and, to some extent, in the character of the Aztecs.

A REMARKABLE MILITARY ALLIANCE

Then was formed that remarkable league, which, indeed, has no parallel in history. It was agreed between the States of Mexico, Tezcuco, and the neighboring little kingdom of Tlacopan that they should mutually support each other in their wars, offensive and defensive, and that in the distribution of the spoil one-fifth should be assigned to Tlacopan and the remainder be divided, in what proportions is uncertain, between the other powers.

What is more extraordinary than the treaty itself, however, is the fidelity with which it was maintained. During a century of uninterrupted warfare that ensued, no instance occurred where the parties quarreled over the division of the spoil, which so often makes shipwreck of similar confederacies among civilized States.

The allies for some time found sufficient occupation for their arms in their own valley; but they soon overleaped its rocky ramparts, and by the middle of the fifteenth century, under the first Montezuma, had spread down the sides of the table-land to the borders of the Gulf of Mexico. Tenochtitlan, the Aztec capital, gave evidence of the public prosperity. Its frail tenements were supplanted by solid structures of stone and lime. Its population rapidly increased.

At the beginning of the sixteenth century, just before the arrival of the Spaniards, the Aztec dominion reached across the continent, from the Atlantic to the Pacific; and, under the bold and bloody Ahuitzotl, its arms had been carried far over the limits already noticed as defining its permanent territory into the farthest corners of Guatemala and Nicaragua. This extent of empire, however limited in comparison with that of many other States, is truly wonderful, considering it as the acquisition of a people whose whole population and resources had so recently been comprised within the walls of their own petty city; and considering, moreover, that the conquered territory was thickly settled by various races, bred to arms like the Mexicans, and little inferior to them in social organization.

THE LAWS OF THE AZTECS

The laws of the Aztecs were registered and exhibited to the people in their hieroglyphical paintings. Much the larger part of them, as in every nation imperfectly civilized, relates rather to the security of persons than of property. The great crimes against society were all made capital. Even the murder of a slave was punished with death.

Thieving, according to the degree of the offense, was punished by slavery or death. Yet the Mexicans could have been under no great apprehension of this crime, since the entrances to their dwellings were not secured by bolts or fastenings of any kind. It was a capital offense to

FORTIFICATIONS AT ACAPULCO, MEXICO

Acapulco is one of the principal west coast cities of Mexico, with harbor accommodations for 100 ocean steamships and 200 lighter craft. Bret Harte, in his "Last Galleon," sings of the day in 1641 when the regular yearly galleon was due to arrive in Acapulco, while the limes were ripening in the sun for the sick on board.

HOUSE IN COUNTRY NEAR CORDOBA

Perhaps three-fourths of Mexico's population has no more of this world's goods than the family in the picture, whose all is contained in this thatched hut and the patch of ground that answers for a garden. Nor does the vast majority know any more than they of creature comforts.

remove the boundaries of another's lands; to alter the established measures, and for a guardian not to be able to give a good account of his ward's property. These regulations evince a regard for equity in dealings and for private rights, which argues a considerable progress in civilization. Prodigals who squandered their patrimony were punished in like manner—a severe sentence, since the crime brought its adequate punishment along with it.

Intemperance, which was the burden, moreover, of their religious homilies, was visited with the severest penalties, as if they had foreseen in it the consuming canker of their own, as well as of the other Indian races in later times. It was punished in the young with death, and in older persons with loss of rank and confiscation of property. Yet a decent conviviality was not meant to be proscribed at their festivals, and they possessed the means of indulging it, in a mild fermented liquor called *pulque*, which is still popular not only with the Indian, but the European population of the country.

STRICT DIVORCE LAWS

The rites of marriage were celebrated with as much formality as in any Christian country, and the institution was held in such reverence that a tribunal was instituted for the sole purpose of determining questions relating to it. Divorces could not be obtained until authorized by a sentence of this court, after a patient hearing of the parties.

But the most remarkable part of the Aztec code was that relating to slavery. There were several descriptions of slaves: prisoners taken in war, who were almost always reserved for the dreadful doom of sacrifice; criminals, public debtors, persons who, from extreme poverty, voluntarily resigned their freedom, and children who were sold by their own parents. In the last instance, usually occasioned also by poverty, it was common for the parents, with the master's consent, to substitute others of their children successively as they grew up, thus distributing the burden as equally as possible among the different members of the family. The willingness of freedom to incur the penalties of this condition is explained by the mild form in which it existed. The contract of sale was executed in the presence of at least four witnesses. The services to be exacted were limited with great precision.

The slave was allowed to have his own family, to hold property, and even other slaves. His children were free. No one could be born to slavery in Mexico; an honorable distinction not known, I believe, in any civilized community where slavery has been sanctioned. Slaves were not sold by their masters, unless when these were driven to it by poverty. They were often liberated by them at their death, and sometimes, were married to them. Yet a refractory or vicious slave might be led into the market, with a collar round his neck, which intimated his bad character, and there be publicly sold, and, on a second sale, reserved for sacrifice.

Communication was maintained with the remotest parts of the country by means of couriers. Post-houses were established on the great roads, about two leagues distant from each other. The courier, bearing his dispatches in the form of a hieroglyphical painting, ran with them to the first station, where they were taken by another messenger and carried forward to the next, and so on till they reached the capital. These couriers, trained from childhood, traveled with incredible swiftness; not four or five leagues an hour, as an old chronicler would make us believe, but with such speed that despatches were carried from 100 to 200 miles a day.

Fresh fish was frequently served at Montezuma's table in 24 hours from the time it had been taken in the Gulf of Mexico, 200 miles from the capital. In this way intelligence of the movements of the royal armies was rapidly brought to court; and the dress of the courier, denoting by its color that of his tidings, spreading joy or consternation in the towns through which he passed.

But the great aim of the Aztec institutions, to which private discipline and public honors were alike directed, was the profession of arms. In Mexico, as in Egypt, the soldier shared with the priest the highest consideration. The king, as we have seen, must be an experienced warrior. The tutelary deity of the Aztecs was the god of war. A great object of their military expeditions was to gather he-

A SECTION OF THE WALLS OF THE RUINS OF XOCHICALCO, MEXICO

"The stones of the crown and surface are laid upon each other without cement and kept in place by their weight alone; and as the sculpture of a figure is seen to run over several of them, there can be no doubt that the work was cut after the pyramid was erected. Stones 7 feet in length by nearly 3 feet in breadth are seen here, and all the great blocks of porphyry which compose the building were brought from a distance and borne up a hill 300 feet high. The superstitious Indians believe that the subterranean rooms of these ruins are inhabited by the ghosts of their ancestors and they resist any attempt to explore them."

catombs of captives for his altars. The soldier who fell in battle was transported at once to the region of ineffable bliss in the bright mansions of the Sun.

THE AZTEC COUNTERPART OF CHRISTIAN CRUSADERS

Every war, therefore, became a crusade; and the warrior, animated by a religious enthusiasm, like that of the early Saracen, or the Christian crusader, was not only raised to contempt of danger, but courted it, for the imperishable crown of martyrdom. Thus we find the same impulse acting in the most opposite quarters of the globe, and the Asiatic, the European, and the American, each earnestly invoking the holy name of religion in the perpetration of human butchery.

The dress of the higher warriors was picturesque and often magnificent. Their bodies were covered with a close vest of quilted cotton, so thick as to be impenetrable to the light missiles of Indian warfare. This garment was so light and serviceable that it was adopted by the Spaniards. The wealthier chiefs sometimes wore, instead of this cotton mail, a cuirass made of thin plates of gold or silver. Over it was thrown a surcoat of the gorgeous feather-work in which they excelled. Their helmets were sometimes of wood, fashioned like the heads of wild animals, and sometimes of silver, on the top of which waved a *panache* of variegated plumes, sprinkled with precious stones and ornaments of gold. They also wore collars, bracelets, and ear-rings of the same rich material.

The national standard, which has been compared to the ancient Roman, displayed, in its embroidery of gold and feather-work, the armorial ensigns of the state. These were significant of its name, which, as the names of both persons and places were borrowed from some material object, was easily expressed by hieroglyphical symbols. The companies and the great chiefs had also their appropriate banners and devices, and the gaudy hues of their many-colored plumes gave a dazzling splendor to the spectacle.

MARCHED SINGING INTO BATTLE

Their tactics were such as belong to a nation with whom war, though a trade, is not elevated to the rank of a science. They advanced singing and shouting their war-cries, briskly charging the enemy, as rapidly retreating, and making use of ambuscades, sudden surprises, and the light skirmish of guerilla warfare. Yet their discipline was such as to draw forth the encomiums of the Spanish Conquerors. "A beautiful sight it was," says one of them, "to see them set out on their march, all moving forward so gayly and in so admirable order!" In battle they did not seek to kill their enemies so much as to take them prisoners, and they never

scalped, like other North American tribes. The valor of a warrior was estimated by the number of his prisoners, and no ransom was large enough to save the devoted captive.

Their military code bore the same stern features as their other laws. Disobedience of orders was punished with death. It was death also for a soldier to leave his colors, to attack the enemy before the signal was given, or to plunder another's booty or prisoners. One of the last Tezcucan princes, in the spirit of an ancient Roman, put two sons to death, after having cured their wounds, for violating the last-mentioned law.

THEIR "HOUSES OF GOD"

The Mexican temples—*teocallis*, "houses of God," as they were called—were very numerous. They were solid masses of earth, cased with brick or stone, and in their form somewhat resemble the pyramidal structures of ancient Egypt. The bases of many of them were more than a hundred feet square, and they towered to a still greater height. They were distributed into four or five stories, each of smaller dimensions than that below. The ascent was by a flight of steps, at an angle of the pyramid, on the outside. This led to a sort of terrace, or gallery, at the base of the second story, which passed quite round the building to another flight of stairs, commencing also at the same angle as the preceding and directly over it, and leading to a similar terrace; so that one had to make the circuit of the temple several times before reaching the summit. In some instances the stairway led directly up the center of the western face of the building.

The top was a broad area, on which were erected one or two towers, 40 or 50 feet high, the sanctuaries in which stood the sacred images of the presiding deities. Before these towers stood the dreadful stone of sacrifice and two lofty altars, on which fires were kept, as inextinguishable as those in the Temple of Vesta. There were said to be 600 of these altars on smaller buildings within the inclosure of the great temple of Mexico, which, with those in the sacred edifices in other parts of the city, shed a brilliant illumination over its streets through the darkest night.

CEREMONIALS OF PEACE

From the construction of their temples all religious services were public. The long processions of priests winding round their massive sides, as they rose higher and higher toward the summit, and the dismal rites of sacrifice performed there, were all visible from the remotest corners of the capital, impressing on the spectator's mind a superstitious veneration for the mysteries of his religion and for the dread ministers by whom they were interpreted.

This impression was kept in full force by their numerous festivals. Every month was consecrated to some protecting deity; and every week—nay, almost every day—was set down in their calendar for some appropriate celebration; so that it is difficult to understand how the ordinary business of life could have been compatible with the exactions of religion. Many of their ceremonies were of a light and cheerful complexion, consisting of the national songs and

ANOTHER VIEW OF THE XOCHICALCO RUINS: CUERNAVACA, MEXICO

Many of the neighboring hacienda houses were built of stone taken from these ruins. The carvings are of warriors, serpents, birds, animals, and plants. At the foot of the hill which these stones surmount are several caves, one known as the Grotto of the Sun.

GIANT CYPRESS AT TULE, NEAR CITY OF OAXACA, MEXICO

This great tree, 154 feet high and its trunk so large that 28 men with outstretched arms can barely encircle it, is one of the largest in the world. Humboldt inscribed his name upon it, and, history says, Cortez rested his men under its branches while en route to Honduras.

STREET OF THE DEAD: SAN JUAN TEOTIHUACAN, MEXICO

The sacred pyramids of San Juan Teotihuacan, situated 27 miles northeast of Mexico City, are reputed to be the largest artificial mounds in the New World. It is believed that they were built at least 900 years before Columbus discovered America.

dances, in which both sexes joined. Processions were made of women and children crowned with garlands and bearing offerings of fruits, the ripened maize, or the sweet incense of copal and other odoriferous gums, while the altars of the deity were stained with no blood save that of animals.

These were the peaceful rites derived from their Toltec predecessors, on which the fierce Aztecs engrafted a superstition too loathsome to be exhibited in all its nakedness, and one over which I would gladly draw a veil altogether, but that it would leave the reader in ignorance of their most striking institution, and one that had the greatest influence in forming the national character.

Human sacrifices were adopted by the Aztecs early in the fourteenth century, about 200 years before the Conquest. Rare at first, they became more frequent with the wider extent of their empire, till at length almost every festival was closed with this cruel abomination. These religious ceremonials were generally arranged in such a manner as to afford a type of the most prominent circumstances in the character or history of the deity who was the object of them. A single example will suffice.

PRISONERS IN THE RÔLES OF GODS

One of their most important festivals was that in honor of the god Tezcatlipoca, whose rank was inferior only to that of the Supreme Being. He was called "the soul of the world," and supposed to have been its creator. He was depicted as a handsome man, endowed with perpetual youth. A year before the intended sacrifice a captive, distinguished for his personal beauty, and without a blemish on his body, was selected to represent this deity. Certain tutors took charge of him and instructed him how to perform his new part with becoming grace and dignity. He was arrayed in a splendid dress, re-

PULQUE GATHERERS NEAR TOLUCA, MEXICO

Toluca is nearly a thousand feet higher than Mexico City, which, in its turn, is a mile and a half higher than Washington or New York. It is too high for dogs, cats, and insects, which are scarcer here than in almost any other city in the country.

AN INDIAN KITCHEN IN HIGHLAND MEXICO

The kind of housekeeping whose story this picture tells is responsible in part for the high death rate in Mexico. If our sanitary conditions and our doctors were no better than those of Mexico, we would have a million deaths a year more than we have now, and not based upon the fortunes of war either.

galed with incense and with a profusion of sweet-scented flowers, of which the ancient Mexicans were as fond as their descendants at the present day.

When he went abroad he was attended by a train of the royal pages, and as he halted in the streets to play some favorite melody the crowd prostrated themselves before him and did him homage as the representative of their good deity. In this way he led an easy, luxurious life, till within a month of his sacrifice. Four beautiful girls, bearing the names of the principal goddesses, were then selected to be his companions, and with them he continued to live in idle dalliance, feasted at the banquets of the princi-

pal nobles, who paid him all the honors of a divinity.

THE FATAL DAY OF SACRIFICE

At length the fatal day of sacrifice arrived. The term of his short-lived glories was at an end. He was stripped of his gaudy apparel and bade adieu to the fair partners of his revelries. One of the royal barges transported him across the lake to a temple which rose on its margin, about a league from the city. Hither the inhabitants of the capital flocked to witness the consummation of the ceremony. As the sad procession wound up the sides of the pyramid, the unhappy victim threw away his gay chaplets of flowers and broke in pieces the musical instruments with which he had solaced the hours of captivity.

On the summit he was received by six priests, whose long and matted locks flowed disorderly over their sable robes, covered with hieroglyphic scrolls of mystic import. They led him to the sacrificial stone, a huge block of jasper, with its upper surface somewhat convex. On this the prisoner was stretched.

Five priests secured his head and his limbs, while the sixth, clad in a scarlet mantle, emblematic of his bloody office, dexterously opened the breast of the wretched victim with a sharp razor of *itzili*—a volcanic substance, hard as flint—and, inserting his hand in the wound, tore out the palpitating heart. The minister of death, first holding this up toward the sun—an object of worship throughout Anahuac—cast it at the feet of the deity to whom the temple was devoted, while the multitudes below prostrated themselves in humble adoration. The tragic story of this prisoner was expounded by the priests as the type of human destiny which, brilliant in its commencement, too often closes in sorrow and disaster.

WOMEN AND CHILDREN OFFERED UP

Such was the form of human sacrifice usually practised by the Aztecs. It was the same that often met the indignant eyes of the Europeans in their progress through the country, and from the dreadful doom of which they themselves were not exempted. There were, indeed, some occasions when preliminary tortures, of the most exquisite kind—with which it is unnecessary to shock the reader—were inflicted, but they always terminated with the bloody ceremony above described. It should be remarked, however, that such tortures were not the spontaneous suggestions of cruelty, as with the North American Indians, but were all rigorously prescribed in the Aztec ritual, and doubtless were often inflicted with the same compunctious visitings which a devout familiar of the Holy Office might at times experience in executing its stern decrees.

Women as well as the other sex were sometimes reserved for sacrifice. On some occasions, particularly in seasons of drought, at the festival of the insatiable Tlaloc, the god of rain, children, for the most part infants, were offered up. As they were borne along in open litters, dressed in their festal robes and decked with the fresh blossoms of spring, they moved the hardest heart to pity, though their cries were drowned in the wild chant of the priests, who read in their tears a favorable augury for their petition. These innocent victims were generally bought by the priests of parents who were poor, but who stifled the voice of nature, probably less at the suggestions of poverty than of a wretched superstition.

CANNIBALS WITH REFINED TASTES

The most loathsome part of the story—the manner in which the body of the sacrificed captive was disposed of—remains yet to be told. It was delivered to the warrior who had taken him in battle, and by him, after being dressed, was served up in an entertainment to his friends. This was not the coarse repast of famished cannibals, but a banquet teeming with delicious beverages and delicate viands, prepared with art and attended by both sexes, who conducted themselves with all the decorum of civilized life. Surely never were refinement and the extreme of barbarism brought so closely in contact with each other!

A MAGUEY PLANT IN BLOOM: MEXICO

A maguey plant in bloom is a sight one seldom sees in Mexico, for the reason that the stem is cut at its base and hollowed out, and the sap that would have gone into the flowers is collected and converted into that evil-smelling, criminal-making concoction called *pulque*. When the sap gathers—at the rate of ten to fifteen pints a day—peons pass from plant to plant, and with their mouths to one end of a tube suck it up, and then discharge it into containers made of pigskins, flung, saddle-bags fashion, across the back of an uncurried donkey. The liquid is then carried to the central station, where it is "ripened" in vats of untanned cowhide.

Human sacrifices have been practised by many nations, not excepting the most polished nations of antiquity, but never by any on a scale to be compared with those in Anahuac.

Agriculture in Mexico was in the same advanced state as the other arts of social life. In few countries, indeed, has it been more respected. It was closely interwoven with the civil and religious institutions of the nation. There were peculiar deities to preside over it; the names of the months and of the religious festivals had more or less reference to it.

Among the most important articles of husbandry we may notice the banana. Another celebrated plant was the cacao, the fruit of which furnished the chocolate—from the Mexican *chocolatl*—now so common a beverage throughout Europe. The vanilla, confined to a small district of the seacoast, was used for the same purposes, of flavoring their food and drink, as with us.

MEAL AND SUGAR FROM MAIZE

The great staple of the country, as, indeed, of the American continent, was maize, or Indian corn, which grew freely along the valleys and up the steep sides of the Cordilleras to the high level of the table-land. The Aztecs were

HIGH-WATER OVEN ON THE TAMESI RIVER, NEAR TAMPICO, MEXICO

The oven is elevated to avoid flooding from the periodic overflows of the river. On the Atlantic slope of Mexico the rainfall is very heavy—from 8 to 12 feet a year—and it often comes in such a downpour as to threaten to wash everything away.

as curious in its preparation and as well instructed in its manifold uses as the most expert New England housewife. Its gigantic stalks, in these equinoctial regions, afford a saccharine matter not found to the same extent in northern latitudes, and supplied the natives with sugar little inferior to that of the cane itself, which was not introduced among them till after the Conquest.

THE MAGUEY'S VERSATILITY

But the miracle of nature was the great Mexican aloe, or *maguey*, whose clustering pyramids of flowers, towering above their dark coronals of leaves, were seen sprinkled over many a broad acre of the table-land. As we have already noticed, its bruised leaves afforded a paste from which paper was manufactured; its juice was fermented into an intoxicating beverage, *pulque*, of which the natives to this day are excessively fond; its leaves further supplied an impenetrable thatch for the more humble dwellings; thread, of which coarse stuffs were made, and strong cords, were drawn from its tough and twisted fibers; pins and needles were made of the thorns at the extremity of its leaves, and the root, when properly cooked, was converted into a palatable and nutritious food. The *agave*, in short, was meat, drink, clothing, and writing materials for the Aztec!

The Mexicans were as well acquainted with the mineral as with the vegetable treasures of their kingdom. Silver, lead, and tin they drew from the mines of Tasco; copper from the mountains of Zacotollan. These were taken not only from the crude masses on the surface, but from veins wrought in the solid rock, into which they opened extensive galleries. In fact, the traces of their labors furnished the best indications for the early Spanish miners. Gold, found

on the surface or gleaned from the beds of rivers, was cast into bars or, in the form of dust, made part of the regular tribute of the southern provinces of the empire. The use of iron, with which the soil was impregnated, was unknown to them. Notwithstanding its abundance, it demands so many processes to prepare it for use that it has commonly been one of the last metals pressed into the service of man.

They found a substitute in an alloy of tin and copper, and with tools made of this bronze could cut not only metals, but, with the aid of a silicious dust, the hardest substances, as basalt, porphyry, amethysts, and emeralds. They fashioned these last, which were found very large, into many curious and fantastic forms. They cast, also, vessels of gold and silver, carving them with their metallic chisels in a very delicate manner. Some of the silver vases were so large that a man could not encircle them with his arms. They imitated very nicely the figures of animals, and, what was extraordinary, could mix the metals in such a manner that the feathers of a bird or the scales of a fish should be alternately of gold and silver. The Spanish goldsmiths admitted their superiority over themselves in these ingenious works.

SHAVING WITH STONE RAZORS

They employed another tool, made of *itztli*, or obsidian, a dark transparent mineral, exceedingly hard, found in abundance in their hills. They made it into knives, razors, and their serrated swords. It took a keen edge, though soon blunted. With this they wrought the various stones and alabasters employed in the construction of their public works and principal dwellings.

The most remarkable piece of sculpture yet disinterred is the great calendar-stone. It con-

THE VOLCANO POPOCATEPETL, FROM THE VALLEY OF MEXICO

In the geography classes in school we are taught to pronounce the name of this beautiful mountain Popo-cat-epetl, putting the emphasis on "cat." The correct way is Popo-ca-tepetl. The Aztec Indians joined the modifying adjective to its noun with a preposition just as we join two nouns or two parts of a compound sentence with a conjunction. The "ca" in the word Popocatepetl is the conjunction which joins "popo," meaning smoking, to "tepetl," meaning hill.

WRECKS ON THE BEACH NEAR VERA CRUZ, MEXICO

And eloquent they are of a form of civilization that spends its energies on internecine war rather than upon the improvement of the lanes of the near-by sea.

sists of dark porphyry, and in its original dimensions as taken from the quarry is computed to have weighed nearly fifty tons. It was transported from the mountains beyond Lake Chalco, a distance of many leagues, over a broken country intersected by water-courses and canals. In crossing a bridge which traversed one of these latter in the capital the supports gave way, and the huge mass was precipitated into the water, whence it was with difficulty recovered. The fact that so enormous a fragment of porphyry could be thus safely carried for leagues, in the face of such obstacles and without the aid of cattle—for the Aztecs, as already mentioned, had no animals of draught—sug-

gests to us no mean ideas of their mechanical skill and of their machinery, and implies a degree of cultivation little inferior to that demanded for the geometrical and astronomical science displayed in the inscriptions on this very stone.

WONDERFUL DYES

The ancient Mexicans made utensils of earthenware for the ordinary purposes of domestic life, numerous specimens of which still exist. They made cups and vases of a lackered or painted wood, impervious to wet and gaudily colored. Their dyes were obtained from both mineral and vegetable substances. Among them was the rich crimson of the cochineal, the modern rival of the famed Tyrian purple. It was introduced into Europe from Mexico, where the curious little insect was nourished with great care on plantations of cactus, since fallen into neglect. The natives were thus enabled to give a brilliant coloring to the webs, which were manufactured of every degree of fineness from the cotton raised in abundance throughout the warmer regions of the country. They had the art, also, of interweaving with these the delicate hair of rabbits and other animals, which made a cloth of great warmth as well as beauty of a kind altogether original, and on this they often laid a rich embroidery of birds, flowers, or some other fanciful device.

But the art in which they most delighted was their *plumaje*, or feather-work. With this they could produce all the effect of a beautiful mosaic. The gorgeous plumage of the tropical birds, especially of the parrot tribe, afforded every variety of color; and the fine down of the humming-bird, which reveled in swarms among the honeysuckle bowers of Mexico, supplied them with soft aërial tints that gave an exquisite finish to the picture. The feathers, pasted on a fine cotton web, were wrought into dresses for the wealthy, hangings for apartments, and ornaments for the temples. No one of the American fabrics excited such admiration in Europe, whither numerous specimens were sent by the Conquerors.

The ancient city of Mexico covered the same spot occupied by the modern capital. The great causeways touched it in the same points; the streets ran in much the same direction, nearly from north to south and from east to west; the cathedral in the *plaza mayor* stands on the same ground that was covered by the temple of the Aztec war-god, and the four principal quarters of the town are still known among the Indians by their ancient names.

Yet an Aztec of the days of Montezuma, could he behold the modern metropolis, which has risen with such phoenix-like splendor from the ashes of the old, would not recognize its site as that of his own Tenochtitlan; for the latter was encompassed by the salt floods of Tezcuco, which flowed in ample canals through every part of the city, while the Mexico of our day stands high and dry on the main land, nearly a league distant at its center from the water. The cause of this apparent change in its position is the diminution of the lake, which, from the rapidity of evaporation in these elevated regions, had become perceptible before the Conquest, but which has since been greatly accelerated by artificial causes.

THE CITY IMMACULATE

A careful police provided for the health and cleanliness of the city. A numerous retinue are said to have been daily employed in watering and sweeping the streets, so that a man—to borrow the language of an old Spaniard—"could walk through them with as little danger of soiling his feet as his hands." The water, in a city washed on all sides by the salt floods, was extremely brackish. A liberal supply of the pure element, however, was brought from Chapultepec, "the grasshopper's hill," less than a league distant. It was brought through an earthen pipe, along a dike constructed for the purpose. That there might be no failure in so essential an article when repairs were going on, a double course of pipes was laid. In this way a column of water of the size of a man's body was conducted into the heart of the capital, where it fed the fountains and reservoirs of the principal mansions. Openings were made in the aque-

WEAVING A BLANKET IN INDIAN MEXICO

The hand-woven blankets made by the Indian girls, to whom a dime a day is a good wage, although they begin work at sunrise and labor until sunset, are the admiration and despair of all who appreciate fine handiwork or value perfect color combinations. A small blanket bought in Mexico City five years ago, although it has been used as a wall tapestry ever since, seems as bright in every one of its rainbow colors as on the day it was bought. The weaving is so perfect that it has no right or wrong side.

duct as it crossed the bridges, and thus a supply was furnished to the canoes below, by means of which it was transported to all parts of the city.

While Montezuma encouraged a taste for architectural magnificence in his nobles, he contributed his own share toward the embellishment of the city. It was in his reign that the famous calendar-stone, weighing, probably, in its primitive state, nearly fifty tons, was transported from its native quarry, many leagues distant, to the capital, where it still forms one of the most curious monuments of Aztec science. Indeed, when we reflect on the difficulty of hewing such a stupendous mass from its hard basaltic bed without the aid of iron tools, and that of transporting it such a distance across land and water without the help of animals, we may well feel admiration at the mechanical ingenuity and enterprise of the people who accomplished it.

MONTEZUMA'S MAGNIFICENT MANSION

Not content with the spacious residence of his father, Montezuma erected another on a yet more magnificent scale. This building, or, as it might more correctly be styled, pile of buildings, spread over an extent of ground so vast that, as one of the Conquerors assures us, its terraced roof might have afforded ample room for thirty knights to run their courses in a regular tourney. Remarkable were its interior decorations, its fanciful draperies, its roofs inlaid with cedar and other odoriferous woods, held together without a nail and, probably, without a knowledge of the arch, its numerous and spacious apartments, which Cortés, with enthusiastic hyperbole, does not hesitate to declare superior to anything of the kind in Spain.

Adjoining the principal edifice were others devoted to various objects. One was an armory, filled with the weapons and military dresses worn by the Aztecs, all kept in the most perfect order, ready for instant use. The emperor was himself very expert in the management of the *maquahuitl*, or Indian sword, and took great delight in witnessing athletic exercises and the mimic representation of war by his young nobility. Another building was used as a granary,

and others as warehouses for the different articles of food and apparel contributed by the districts charged with the maintenance of the royal household.

There were also edifices appropriated to objects of quite another kind. One of these was an immense aviary, in which birds of splendid plumage were assembled from all parts of the empire. Here was the scarlet cardinal, the golden pheasant, the endless parrot tribe, with their rainbow hues (the royal green predominant), and that miniature miracle of nature, the humming-bird, which delights to revel among the honeysuckle bowers of Mexico. Three hundred attendants had charge of this aviary, who made themselves acquainted with the appropriate food of its inmates, oftentimes procured at great cost, and in the moulting season were careful to collect the beautiful plumage, which, with its many-colored tints, furnished the materials for the Aztec painter.

A separate building was reserved for the fierce birds of prey; the voracious vulture tribes and eagles of enormous size, whose home was in the snowy solitudes of the Andes. No less than five hundred turkeys, the cheapest meat in Mexico, were allowed for the daily consumption of these tyrants of the feathered race.

THE AZTEC ZOO DESCRIBED

Adjoining this aviary was a menagerie of wild animals, gathered from the mountain forests, and even from the remote swamps of the *tierra caliente*.

The collection was still further swelled by a great number of reptiles and serpents remarkable for their size and venomous qualities, among which the Spaniards beheld the fiery little animal "with the castanets in his tail," the terror of the American wilderness. The serpents were confined in long cages lined with down or feathers or in troughs of mud and water.

The beasts and birds of prey were provided with apartments large enough to allow of their moving about, and secured by a strong lattice-work, through which light and air were freely admitted. The whole was placed under the charge of numerous keepers, who acquainted themselves with the habits of their prisoners and provided for their comfort and cleanliness.

With what deep interest would the enlightened naturalist of that day—an Oviedo, or a Martyr, for example—have surveyed this magnificent collection, in which the various tribes which roamed over the Western wilderness, the unknown races of an unknown world, were brought into one view! How would they have delighted to study the peculiarities of these new species, compared with those of their own hemisphere, and thus have risen to some comprehension of the general laws by which Nature acts in all her works! The rude followers of Cortés did not trouble themselves with such refined speculations. They gazed on the spectacle with a vague curiosity not unmixed with awe, and as they listened to the wild cries of the ferocious animals and the hissings of the serpents they almost fancied themselves in the infernal regions.

MOUNTAIN ROAD: SAN MIGUEL DE ALLENDE, MEXICO

Good roads in Mexico are about as rare as good men in a den of thieves, and this is one of the exceptions. Under the Diaz regime railroad building was the principal activity of the country. Since then its energies have been too absorbed with revolutions and counter-revolutions to leave any time for highway improvement.

A ROYAL MUSEUM OF HUMAN FREAKS

I must not omit to notice a strange collection of human monsters, dwarfs, and other unfortunate persons, in whose organization Nature had capriciously deviated from her regular laws. Such hideous anomalies were regarded by the Aztecs as a suitable appendage of state. It is even said they were in some cases the result of artificial means, employed by unnatural parents desirous to secure a provision for their offspring by thus qualifying them for a place in the royal museum!

Extensive gardens were spread out around these buildings, filled with fragrant shrubs and flowers, and especially with medicinal plants. No country has afforded more numerous species of these last than New Spain, and their virtues were perfectly understood by the Aztecs, with whom medical botany may be said to have been studied as a science. Amidst this labyrinth of sweet-scented groves and shrubberies fountains of pure water might be seen throwing up their sparkling jets and scattering refreshing dews over the blossoms. Ten large tanks, well stocked with fish, afforded a retreat on their margins to various tribes of waterfowl, whose habits were so carefully consulted that some of these ponds were of salt water, as that which they most loved to frequent. A tessellated pavement of marble inclosed the ample basins which were overhung by light and fanciful pavilions, that admitted the perfumed breezes of the gardens and offered a grateful shelter to the monarch in the sultry heats of summer.

FASHIONS IN ANCIENT AZTEC-LAND

The Spaniards were struck, on entering the capital, with the appearance of the inhabitants and their great superiority in the style and quality of their dress over the people of the lower countries. The *tilmatli* or cloak thrown over the shoulders and tied round the neck, made of cotton of different degrees of fineness, according to the condition of the wearer, and the ample sash around the loins, were often wrought in rich and elegant figures and edged with a deep fringe or tassel. As the weather was now growing cool, mantles of fur or of the gorgeous feather-work were sometimes substituted. The latter combined the advantage of great warmth with beauty. The Mexicans had also the art of spinning a fine thread of the hair of the rabbit and other animals, which they wove into a delicate web that took a permanent dye.

The women, as in other parts of the country, seemed to go about as freely as the men. They wore several skirts or petticoats of different lengths, with highly ornamented borders, and sometimes over them loose flowing robes, which reached to the ankles. These, also, were made of cotton, for the wealthier classes, of a fine texture, prettily embroidered. The Aztec women had their faces exposed, and their dark, raven tresses floated luxuriantly over their shoulders, revealing features which, although of a dusky or rather cinnamon hue, were not unfrequently pleasing.

A REMARKABLE MARKET-PLACE

On drawing near to the *tianguez*, or great market, the Spaniards were astonished at the throng of people pressing toward it, and, on entering the place, their surprise was still further heightened by the sight of the multitudes assembled there and the dimensions of the inclosure, thrice as large as the celebrated square of Salamanca. Here were met together traders from all parts, with the products and manufactures peculiar to their countries—the goldsmiths

COCK FIGHT: RANCH NEAR LEON, MEXICO

It is a customary sight to walk along the streets of a rural Mexican town and see game cocks tethered at every front door or to see a train stop at a station with fighting roosters perched in most of the windows of the peon coaches, each one held by his owner.

of Azcapozalco, the potters and jewelers of Cholula, the painters of Tezcuco, the stonecutters of Tenajocan, the hunters of Xilotepec, the fishermen of Cuitlahuac, the fruiterers of the warm countries, the mat and chair makers of Quauhtitlan, and the florists of Xochimilco—all busily engaged in recommending their respective wares and in chaffering with purchasers.

IN THE TOY SHOP

The market-place was surrounded by deep porticos, and the several articles had each its own quarter allotted to it. Here might be seen cotton piled up in bales, or manufactured into dresses and articles of domestic use, as tapestry, curtains, coverlets, and the like. The richly stained and nice fabrics reminded Cortés of the *alcay-cería*, or silk-market of Granada. There was the quarter assigned to the goldsmiths, where the purchaser might find various articles of ornament or use formed of the precious metals, or curious toys, made in imitation of birds and fishes, with scales and feathers alternately of gold and silver and with movable heads and bodies. These fantastic little trinkets were often garnished with precious stones, and showed a patient, puerile ingenuity in the manufacture, like that of the Chinese.

In an adjoining quarter were collected specimens of pottery, coarse and fine, vases of wood elaborately carved, varnished, or gilt, of curious and sometimes graceful forms. There

FIGHTING COCKS: QUERÉTARO, MEXICO

The peon with Spanish blood in his veins is nearly always fond of the sight of gore. At a Mexican cockpit the betting is faster and more furious than the fun at a three-ring circus, and the enthusiasm is about as great when the steel-spurred cocks cut one another to pieces as when a mad bull gores a horse to death in the bull-ring. Moral sense, after all, it would seem, is largely a question of geography.

were also hatchets made of copper alloyed with tin, the substitute, and, as it proved, not a bad one for iron. The soldier found here all the implements of his trade. The casque fashioned into the head of some wild animal, with its grinning defenses of teeth and bristling crest dyed with the rich tint of the cochineal; the *escaupil*, or quilted doublet of cotton, the rich surcoat of feather-mail, and weapons of all sorts, copper-headed lances and arrows, and the broad *maquahuitl*, the Mexican sword, with its sharp blades of *itztli*. Here were razors and mirrors of this same hard and polished mineral which served so many of the purposes of steel with the Aztecs.

In the square were also to be found booths occupied by barbers, who used these same razors in their vocation; for the Mexicans, contrary to the popular and erroneous notions respecting the Aborigines of the New World, had beards, though scanty ones. Other shops or booths were tenanted by apothecaries, well provided with drugs, roots, and different medicinal preparations. In other places, again, blank books or maps for the hieroglyphical picture-writing were to be seen, folded together like fans and made of cotton, skins, or more commonly the fibers of the agave, the Aztec papyrus.

Under some of the porticos they saw hides, raw and dressed, and various articles for domestic or personal use made of the leather. Animals, both wild and tame, were offered for sale, and near them, perhaps, a gang of slaves, with collars round their necks, intimating they were likewise on sale—a spectacle, unhappily, not confined to the barbarian markets of Mexico, though the evils of their condition were aggravated there by the consciousness that a life of degradation might be consummated at any moment by the dreadful doom of sacrifice.

SAVORY DISHES READY TO SERVE

The heavier materials for building, as stone, lime, timber, were considered too bulky to be allowed a place in the square, and were deposited in the adjacent streets on the borders of the canals. It would be tedious to enumerate all the various articles, whether for luxury or daily use, which were collected from all quarters in this vast bazaar. I must not omit to mention, however, the display of provisions, one of the most attractive features of the *tianguez*; meats of all kinds, domestic poultry, game from the neighboring mountains, fish from the lakes and streams, fruits in all the delicious abundance of these temperate regions, green vegetables, and the unfailing maize. There was many a viand, too, ready dressed, which sent up its savory steams, provoking the appetite of the idle passenger; pastry, bread of the Indian corn, cakes, and confectionery. Along with these were to be seen cooling or stimulating beverages, the spicy foaming *chocolatl*, with its delicate aroma of vanilla, and the inebriating *pulque*, the fermented juice of the aloe. All these commodities, and every stall and portico, were set out, or rather smothered, with flowers, showing, on a much greater scale, indeed, a taste similar to that displayed in the markets of modern Mexico.

The most perfect order reigned throughout this vast assembly.

The women partook equally with the men of social festivities and entertainments. These were often conducted on a large scale, both as regards the number of guests and the costliness of the preparations. Numerous attendants, of both sexes, waited at the banquet. The halls were scented with perfumes and the courts strewed with odoriferous herbs and flowers, which were distributed in profusion among the

Photograph by John H. Hall

A PUBLIC SCRIBE: MEXICO

For four centuries the Spaniards and their descendants have ruled Mexico, but the ratio of illiteracy to literacy is little changed since Cortez brought the Indians under the yoke of Castile and Aragon.

guests as they arrived. Cotton napkins and ewers of water were placed before them as they took their seats at the board; for the venerable ceremony of ablution, before and after eating, was punctiliously observed by the Aztecs.

SNUFF USED IN TENOCHTITLAN

Tobacco was then offered to the company, in pipes, mixed up with aromatic substances, or in the form of cigars, inserted in tubes of tortoise shell or silver. They compressed the nostrils with the fingers while they inhaled the smoke, which they frequently swallowed. Whether the women, who sat apart from the men at table, were allowed the indulgence of the fragrant weed, as in the most polished circles of modern Mexico, is not told us. It is a curious fact that the Aztecs also took the dried leaf in the pulverized form of snuff.

The table was well provided with substantial meats, especially game, among which the most conspicuous was the turkey, erroneously

POPOCATEPETL FROM THE SUMMIT OF THE IXTACCIHUATL

This graceful extinct volcano rises more than three miles above the level of the sea. According to Indian traditions, it came into being after a violent earthquake following terrific subterranean noises. It has been quiescent since 1802. Statisticians estimate that 100,000,000 pounds of sulphur have been removed from it since the Conquest.

supposed, as its name imports, to have come originally from the East. These more solid dishes were flanked by others of vegetables and fruits, of every delicious variety found on the North American continent. The different viands were prepared in various ways, with delicate sauces and seasoning, of which the Mexicans were very fond. Their palate was still further regaled by confections and pastry, for which their maize flour and sugar supplied ample materials.

The meats were kept warm by chafing-dishes. The table was ornamented with vases of silver, and sometimes gold, of delicate workmanship. The drinking cups and spoons were of the same costly materials, and likewise of tortoise shell. The favorite beverage was the *chocolatl*, flavored with vanilla and different spices. They had a way of preparing the froth of it so as to make it almost solid enough to be eaten and took it cold. The fermented juice of the maguey, with a mixture of sweets and acids, supplied also various agreeable drinks, of different degrees of strength, and formed the chief beverage of the elder part of the company.

CRITICISING THE HOST

As soon as they had finished their repast, the young people rose from the table, to close the festivities of the day with dancing. They danced gracefully to the sound of various in-

A NATURE'S BATH-TUB AT CUERNAVACA, MEXICO

There are probably fewer bath-tubs in all tropical America than there are in the single city of New York. "The old swimming-hole" must answer for many millions of Mexicans; and in Mexico swimming-holes are often many miles apart.

struments, accompanying their movements with chants of a pleasing, though somewhat plaintive, character. The older guests continued at table, sipping *pulque* and gossiping about other times, till the virtues of the exhilarating beverage put them in good humor with their own.

Intoxication was not rare in this part of the company, and, what is singular, was excused in them, though severely punished in the younger. The entertainment was concluded by a liberal distribution of rich dresses and ornaments among the guests, when they withdrew, after midnight, "some commending the feast and others condemning the bad taste or ex-

travagance of their host; in the same manner," says an old Spanish writer, "as with us." Human nature is indeed much the same all the world over.

We shall be able to form a better idea of the actual refinement of the natives by penetrating into their domestic life. We have, fortunately, the means of doing so. We shall there find the ferocious Aztec frequently displaying all the sensibility of a cultivated nature, consoling his friends under affliction, or congratulating them on their good fortune, as on occasion of a marriage or of the birth or baptism of a child, when he was punctilious in his visits, bringing presents of costly dresses and ornaments, or the more simple offering of flowers, equally indicative of his sympathy. The visits at these times, though regulated with all the precision of Oriental courtesy, were accompanied by expressions of the most cordial and affectionate regard.

In this remarkable picture of manners, which I have copied faithfully from the records of earliest date after the Conquest, we find no resemblance to the other races of North American Indians. Some resemblance we may trace to the general style of Asiatic pomp and luxury. But in Asia woman, far from being admitted to unreserved intercourse with the other sex, is too often jealously immured within the walls of the harem.

The Aztec character was perfectly original and unique. It was made up of incongruities apparently irreconcilable. It blended into one the marked peculiarities of different nations, not only of the same phase of civilization, but as far removed from each other as the extremes of barbarism and refinement. It may find a fitting parallel in their own wonderful climate, capable of producing, on a few square leagues of surface, the boundless variety of vegetable forms, which belong to the frozen regions of the North, the temperate zone of Europe, and the burning skies of Arabia and Hindostan!

FURTHER READING

MAYA

Linda Schele, a pioneer in the study of the Maya, collaborated on a series of important books, among them *A Forest of Kings: The Untold Story of the Maya* (1990); *The Blood of Kings: Dynasty and Ritual in Maya Art* (1986) and *The Code of Kings* (1998). See also George C. Stuart, *The Mysterious Maya* (1977); Sylvanus G. Marley, *The Ancient Maya* (1983) and Norman Hammond, *Ancient Maya Civilization* (1994). The latter is a very good summary of Maya archaeology. Younger readers should consult Jacqueline Greene, *The Maya* (1992) and Pamela Odijk, *The Mayas* (1989).

AZTEC

Nigel Davies, *The Aztecs: A History* (1980) and *The Aztec Empire* (1987) are excellent and well-written studies. See also Inga Clendinnen, *Aztecs* (1991) and Richard Townsend, *The Aztecs* (1992). Younger readers should consult Tim Wood, *The Aztecs* (1992).

INDEX

CONTRIBUTORS

General Editor FRED L. ISRAEL is an award-winning historian. He received the Scribe's Award from the American Bar Association for his work on the Chelsea House series *The Justices of the United States Supreme Court*. A specialist in American history, he was general editor for Chelsea's *1897 Sears Roebuck Catalog*. Dr. Israel has also worked in association with Arthur M. Schlesinger, Jr. on many projects, including *The History of the U.S. Presidential Elections* and *The History of U.S. Political Parties*. He is senior consulting editor on the Chelsea House series *Looking into the Past: People, Places, and Customs*, which examines past traditions, customs, and cultures of various nations.

Senior Consulting Editor ARTHUR M. SCHLESINGER, JR. is the pre-eminent American historian of our time. He won the Pulitzer Prize for his book *The Age of Jackson* (1945), and again for *A Thousand Days* (1965). This chronicle of the Kennedy Administration also won a National Book Award. He has written many other books, including a multi-volume series, *The Age of Roosevelt*. Professor Schlesinger is the Albert Schweitzer Professor of the Humanities at the City University of New York, and has been involved in several other Chelsea House projects, including the *American Statesmen* series of biographies on the most prominent figures of early American history.